CW00495786

WORK
MADE
EASY

PARTHAJEET SARMA
JOHN HOFFMIRE
RAJ KRISHNAMURTHY

WORK
MADE
EASY

A GUIDE TO SUCCESS IN
HYBRID ENVIRONMENTS

First published by Westland Business, an imprint of Westland Books, a division of Nasadiya Technologies Private Limited, in 2024

No. 269/2B, First Floor, 'Irai Arul', Vimalraj Street, Nethaji Nagar, Alapakkam Main Road, Maduravoyal, Chennai 600095

Westland, the Westland logo, Westland Business and the Westland Business logo are the trademarks of Nasadiya Technologies Private Limited, or its affiliates.

ISBN: 9789360453268

10 9 8 7 6 5 4 3 2 1

Typeset by SÜRYA, New Delhi

Printed at Parksons Graphics Pvt. Ltd

Contents

Introduction   *ix*

Part 1 | THE WHY

I. THE POWER OF EXPERIENCES   3

  1. Experiences vs Things   3
  2. A Post-Materialistic Life   10
  3. An Experience-Based Society   15

II. THE WORKPLACE EXPERIENCE   21

  1. Experiencing Workplaces   21
  2. Employees' Voices Matters   31
  3. What Are Employees Asking For?   37
  4. The Employers' Response   42
  5. Change Management   50

III. A DIFFERENT WORKPLACE JOURNEY   60

  1. The Rise of Worktech   60
  2. Uneasy Workplace Journey   72
  3. Future of Worktech and the Metaverse   78
  4. The Metaverse's Impact on Employee Expectations   93

IV. MAKING IT EASY   99

  1. The Importance of Shifting the Focus   99
  2. Changing Behaviours   107
  3. Persuasive Design   114

V. A DATA-DRIVEN APPROACH   127

  1. The Employee as a Customer   127
  2. Defining the Path to Easy Work   135

Part 2 | THE HOW

VI. PREPARING THE ORGANISATION   143

   1. Refer to the Vision and the Mission   143
   2. Set Up Goals and a Team   145
   3. Take the Design-thinking Approach   150
   4. Ensure Roles Are Understood   153
   5. Remember the Five Steps   156

VII. RESEARCH   160

   1. Collate Small Data   160
   2. Collate Big Data   167

VIII. RECOGNISE   174

   1. Draw Insights from Data   174
   2. Define the Problem Correctly   180

IX. IDEATE   183

   1. Establish Strategy Direction   183
   2. Take an Integrated Approach to Workplace Design   188

X. PILOT   195

   1. Pilot the Workplace Transformation   195
   2. Manage the Change   200
   3. Integrate and Automate Building Services   207
   4. Integrate Productivity and Collaboration Tools   211
   5. Integrate Food and Transportation Tools   214
   6. Complete Pulse Studies and Course Corrections   220
   7. Accumulate User Data To Help Personalise Experiences   223

XI. IMPLEMENT   226

   1. Roll Out   226
   2. Revitalise   229

Conclusion   231

References   234
Index   241
About the Authors   246

Introduction

Artificial Intelligence (AI) tools such as ChatGPT have made writing easier in recent months. When one gets used to ChatGPT, putting together material for websites or reports the conventional way may feel like a huge effort. Similarly, when knowledge workers feel they can get their work done from the comfort of their favourite sofa at home, the trip to the office may feel cumbersome. Managing such shifts in mindset becomes the responsibility of the organisational management. This book is about making it easier to integrate the digital workplace and the physical workplace.

Just as AI is shaking up systems and careers in 2024 and beyond, the way we work is also going through some major changes, especially after the COVID-19 pandemic. It's a big deal, and we need to take a closer look and understand all the different aspects. The old-fashioned ways of working are making room for new ways, and some of the most significant shifts are likely to be on account of AI. AI isn't just about making work easy; if used cleverly, it can also make workplaces and organisations more sustainable and efficient, truly walking the talk rather than just making a corporate statement. But here's the catch: thinking AI will work alone is a mistake. It's going to work hand in hand with many other things, some of which are essentially human. This prompted us to reflect, particularly on the significance of linking various aspects, leading us to write this book.

Your authors live on two different continents and have different professional interests. Individually, we have lived in megacities as well as in small towns. While big cities have enabled us to grow professionally and develop a network of clients and business associates, we are not wed to the metropolitan lifestyle. With fast internet connecting every part of the world, we see merit in living in the periphery of big cities or in smaller nearby towns. The combination of access to the big city and relief from traffic woes give us all the benefits we need. Of course, smaller towns allow more space for gardening, walking in nature and so on. They have no particular disadvantages related to our continuing our professional interests.

But we don't dismiss the feelings of those who love living in urban areas. Living in big cities has many advantages—the cultural attributes of the place, great food, ease of access to good airports, better healthcare and many other benefits. Despite such benefits, these areas can be quite a grapple with relentless crowds, traffic snarls, high costs and constant hustle, making daily existence challenging. But since Uber and its competitors were born, life has become simpler for those living in big cities. Getting around has become easier, as parking worries have reduced. The likes of Deliveroo and Uber Eats have made dinners easy for young working adults and anyone unwilling to cook. Amazon and others have made shopping easy. Airbnb has made short-stay accommodation cheaper. Things have become more accessible to all through mobile apps. As a result, life in the city became somewhat easier on several fronts over the last two decades.

And then came the COVID-19 pandemic. People got used to doing things the easy way. If they could conduct meetings with a flick of their fingers, they would rather do that than travel all the way to the office. Besides other things, the pandemic also shepherded millions of professionals online. People who hardly used email were forced to spend a lot more time on their computers.

The pandemic eventually tapered off, but the online habits did not. Employer organisations are now struggling to wean their people off online meetings and collaborations. Many are expecting their employees to be physically present in the office once again, but employees are pushing back.

Pre-pandemic, the routine for people was to spend their week in the office. During the pandemic, work was mostly only online. There's a middle ground now—welcome to the world of hybrid work, commonly understood as one that combines in-office working with remote working.

The routine of the pre-pandemic day might probably never come back. There are fewer clear patterns or routines now.

Although remote work is more acceptable today than before, and nearly every knowledge worker has access to easier ways of accomplishing tasks, remotely or from the office, the lack of clear patterns makes it difficult to navigate a work day. At the same time, humans like patterns. This is partly because they breed familiarity. The brain is wired to reject the unfamiliar. People even resign from jobs because it is not easy to navigate work weeks and work months riddled with unpredictability and the uncertainty of hybrid work. Most progressive organisations today allow their employees to choose their 'days in office' during a week. The flipside to this is that unlike earlier, the average hybrid worker now cannot easily predict or know which of his close team members will be in office on a certain day of the week. Diet and fitness regimens need constant rejigs to adapt to changing work-week schedules. For a lot of people, each week needs a reset these days, as against the predictable weeks earlier.

During and after the pandemic, as the world adjusted to new

ways of working, corporate leaders have spent months and millions of dollars on the betterment of their people. Employees are being given flexibility about how, when and where they want to work. They are being given a variety of choices, especially on the wellness side. There is a stress on more effective training as well as better communication between the management and employees.

These changes have been championed by many of the great employers with the hope that employees will be motivated to stick around, rather than leaving for another company or a different career path. There is a rush to attract and retain scarce talent, as there is more and more churn in the market and employees move from job to job.

Employers are listening to their employees, analysing what they say in conjunction with the corporate mission and giving them choices and flexibility.

With greater flexibility allowed to employees becoming a norm, adverse consequences result from the opposite—when employees quit to join competitors that offer greater choice and flexibility. While giving people choices and flexibility is most welcome, we have to remember that change is hard. Humans are not wired to absorb changes too often and tend to push back against them, no matter how well-communicated they may be. This is because change brings the unfamiliar, a territory that is often easy to reject.

Change requires the human brain to spend energy getting familiar with it. We are wired to take the path of least resistance, and the moment it becomes easy to do something, we do it. If we can do without spending energy on something, we choose that path. That is why people began buying more things online when Amazon introduced the one-click buy option. That is also why people began taking more cab rides when they could book cabs easily via an app instead of going through the hassle of making multiple calls to coordinate locations and payments.

Employees, especially in early stages of their professional careers, do not behave very differently when it comes to decisions around their current job as opposed to a new one. When changes are introduced within a current role that comes with the need to pick up new skills or require more effort than before, with benefits that mean little to the employee, they often push back. At this point, if an employee has another job offer with the promise of greater choice and flexibility, they might take that rather than go through the changes in their current job. The way around this for employers is to focus on making things easier for employees, rather than focusing on making change.

Often the question is: how do we change things? Instead, the question should be: How do we make things easier? With this change in perspective, the entire ecosystem surrounding the stakeholders shifts. The outlook switches as well and workplace transformation initiatives become more successful.

Human action comes about as the result of two factors working together at the same time: mental comfort and ease of use. From an evolutionary perspective, familiarity leads to comfort. People see things as easy when they are dealing with the familiar. We refer to this as relatability. 'Ease of use' describes how easily users can perform an action. Anything that takes less time, costs less money and requires less physical activity will be considered easier.

Successful social media platforms and AI-integrated digital platforms are built on the back of the understanding that people will take action if they find relatability and ease of use in the things they do. So the good platforms show you more of what you are familiar with or relate to. They collate data about your past choices, build a digital profile of you and push suggestions and content that you are likely to enjoy and engage with. The great platforms make it very easy for you to perform the action you want to complete—possibly through the simple tap of a finger.

The same principles are being used to build the metaverse, which is an immersive virtual world facilitated by the use of virtual reality and augmented reality tools. These concepts can integrate into the world of work too. The current ways of virtual working and collaboration are likely to fuse into metaverses in which employees work virtually. This integration will work well because the metaverse experience will be personalised, nudging us to do things that we are familiar with and with ease. It will feel like a safe and easy world to be in.

The trouble is that employees cannot do everything virtually today. People need people. They need to navigate the physical world and show up in the office on certain days to do human things like socialise, enjoy the smell of coffee or receive a pat on the back. As individuals' expectations of relatability increase and easy-to-use technologies become more present in the virtual world, similar expectations of ease and relatability will build up in the physical world. If the non-virtual experience of employees at work does not measure up to what they can accomplish virtually, work will simply become more difficult to navigate.

Personalised experiences, which feel easy to navigate, can be delivered if employees are understood at a human level. Their needs, aspirations and behaviours need to be appreciated. This requires access to data about such aspects. Big data, like desk-occupancy patterns picked up by sensors or behavioural trends picked up from employee apps, come in handy. Employee apps—which began as smartphone applications to facilitate communication, collaboration and engagement within a workplace—are expanding towards becoming a one-stop shop for everything related to work, including booking seats, meals and parking spots. Small data derived from people interventions such as surveys and interviews are equally important. Analysis and synthesis of both types of data provide credible evidence, with insights drawn from such evidence facilitating decision-making about making things easier. This works well because organisations like to make decisions based on evidence.

Used in marketing and business contexts, a customer experience journey is the end-to-end interaction a customer has with a brand, shaping perceptions and satisfaction. If an employee is looked at with similar lenses, an employee experience journey can be said to be his/her progression across different organisational touchpoints, throughout his or her days within the organisation. Leaders need to reimagine the **employee workplace journey** as one comprising navigation of both the virtual as well as the physical world. For this to happen, the focus of managers needs to shift to delivering easier, more relatable ways of getting things done at every touchpoint in the hybrid workplace journey. This book is about making work easier as employees transition between virtual and physical worlds.

Although AI will play a part in doing so, it's important to note that AI comes at a cost. Predictions suggest that by 2030, AI might use up to 3.5 per cent of the world's electricity. In 2024, the conversation has shifted towards finding a middle ground—utilising smaller AI models to cut costs while leveraging AI for enhanced efficiency in organisations and workplaces. Having witnessed the era of carbon-conscious operations in businesses, we strongly believe in the significance of acting responsibly.

Our book is made up of two parts. While Part 1 is about the

importance and effectiveness of making work easier, Part 2 presents action items for the workplace. Part 1 is about the why and Part 2 is about the how. We want our book to be useful. So, in Part 2, we have given you a list of actionable steps for your workplace.

The list is presented in chronological order because we want you to imagine yourself undertaking a workplace transformation project and going through the steps in the order you would approach them. Each chapter title begins with a verb. And we expect that if you follow these steps, you will have an easier place to work in. We are not saying it will be easy to change your work culture or processes. But we are saying that our suggestions will make it easier.

As you contemplate these steps, think about who you want to involve in the process of leading change in your organisation. The answer may be that the perfect person exists in your entity to do the work, or a decision about how to staff your change management project may be dictated by an organisational chart. If yours is a small entity, you may find that choosing change champions is dictated by the cultural positions that people hold within your organisation as well as their personality. On the other hand, in a bigger organisation, it may be important to include people who, through their titles or their cultural position, can represent and touch the lives of employees across the various layers of the organisation.

The choice is yours. But as you read our book you will notice that we will be making suggestions on how to implement change and who should be involved in this.

At the end of this introduction, we want to address a weakness of the English language. We have felt confined as we have addressed the different types of workers who exist in the world. Our book is mostly about what used to be called white-collar workers. Now, almost no one uses this nomenclature. Instead, some people use the words: knowledge workers. This category connotes technological capacity, specialist skills and aptitude. At the same time, we know that every worker possesses knowledge. It would be condescending to not acknowledge this. At the same time, however, we don't have other terms that work. So, we use both: white-collar workers and knowledge workers. We look forward to the day when someone else can address this issue in a more effective way.

—Parthajeet, John and Raj

Part 1 | THE WHY

THE POWER OF EXPERIENCES

Experiences vs Things

Two of this book's co-authors first met at the University of Oxford, in the United Kingdom, one as a student and the other as his professor. In one of our early catch-ups, we went on a long walk across the valleys and woods around the university, crossing streams on the way, talking about a wide variety of things. After a few hours, we ended up in an eighteenth-century pub. We still remember that day vividly. On the other hand, the former student and the third author met for the first time in a gathering of people with similar business ideas. In the short span of two hours, the two of them exchanged ideas, which glued them together for years to come. The memories of those two hours stay vivid too.

Although the three of us are different from each other, we have a common love of hiking. Individually, whenever time permits, we venture out on hikes with colleagues, friends and family, often in regions without mobile phone connectivity. We have slept in tents in brutal weather, drunk from streams, sung, joked and lived life. These moments, these experiences we lived through, will remain etched in our memories, perhaps for the rest of our lives, incapable of being copied and unlikely to be repeated.

Most of us have memories associated with some of our basic

human needs, like food. We vividly remember that time when hunger pangs got the better of us or another when we shared a meal with friends. When you wake up hungry in the middle of the night and make a trip to the fridge to get something to eat, you are trying to satisfy your body's physiological need. Alternatively, when you are having dinner in a fancy restaurant, you are there for the experience. The aromas, the sights, the sounds—the entire ambience—work together to create an experience that satisfies both the psychological and the physiological parts of your being. Both these scenarios involve the act of eating but fulfil two different human needs.

This is what some experience designers do for a living. They create experiences that centre around the user, drawing from his or her needs, feelings, context and mindset. For example, they plan fast-tempo music in pubs compared with slow, lounge music in fine-dining restaurants. The fast music makes patrons gulp down mug after mug of beer quickly, thereby making the cash register ring. On the other hand, the slow music in fine-dining restaurants contributes to making diners linger and perhaps order multiple courses. Music is one of several key ingredients in designing experiences. Experience design primarily involves the interplay of the five human senses of sight, touch, smell, taste and hearing, and their effect on the user.

When it comes to music, highly popular musicians make more money from concert ticket sales than from album sales. Popular youth icon and musician Taylor Swift is reported to have made $370 million from her much-touted Eras Tour of 2023. The same tour is reported to have pumped a staggering $4.3 billion into the US economy in 2023, according to Bloomberg.

Tracing back a few years, in an article in *Business Insider*, Zach Bellas, a professional musician and founder of American

SMB Records, indicated that leading rock band U2 earned $54.4 million in 2017 and was the highest-paid musical act of the year. Touring accounted for about 95 per cent, or $52 million, of their total earnings. Album sales and streaming made up less than 4 per cent. In second place that year was Garth Brooks, who made 89 per cent of his earnings through touring. Heavy metal band Metallica ranked third; they raked in 71 per cent of their earnings in the same way.[1]

One often hears of illegal downloads being blamed for musicians receiving less money for recorded music. While this may be partially true, what one cannot ignore is that people are not as willing to pay for music in the form of a tangible product anymore. In an Uberised age, what matters is the music experience, not the ownership. The average price of a ticket to the 100 most popular tours in North America has almost quadrupled over the past two decades, from $25 in 1996 to over $100. Concert prices have far outpaced inflation. The average ticket price of Taylor Swift's Eras Tour concerts hovered around $450 in 2023. People pay such prices because they get something they can't get elsewhere. In the mind of a music lover, attending a concert by popular K-Pop band BTS is a one-of-a-kind experience.

In fact, we all know that experience matters, don't we? That is why we visit new places, go to live shows, go hiking in the mountains. Most people are wired to constantly look for new experiences, especially ones they can relate to. So, although a hike in the mountains sounds tough, we may do it, either because we have done it before and are familiar with what it takes or because our best friends are coming along and we enjoy being with people we are familiar with, or a combination of both. At the same time, we crave for novelty in experiences that we are familiar with; that is why bikers keep on looking for new routes, as do mountaineers.

Novelty Seekers

Why do people seek novelty? It is because we are inherently curious. Neuroscience research suggests novelty is powerful because, in evolutionary terms, we pay attention to what's new to determine whether it is a threat. If it is perceived as a threat, the potential experience is rejected. If not, we want to know more. Neuroscientist Dr Emrah Duzel's research suggests that novelty triggers the release of the happy hormone dopamine in the brain as a reward, encouraging us to seek out more. Social media platforms regularly update their algorithms to exploit this, encouraging users to scroll for newer content about topics or people we are familiar with.[2, 3]

Our day-to-day life experiences comprise activities that, when combined together, form routine and breed familiarity. We get up in the morning, brush our teeth, get a coffee, drive to the office, get another coffee and so on. These are things we can do without thinking; the mind and the body work in unison, almost as if we are on autopilot.

However, the things we do outside this routine usually attract our attention. These experiences stand out.

Belle Beth Cooper, in *Novelty and the Brain: Why New Things Make Us Feel So Good*, writes: 'There's a region in our midbrain called the substantia nigra/ventral segmental area or SN/VTA. This is essentially the major "novelty center" of the brain, which responds to novel stimuli. The SN/VTA is closely linked to areas of the brain called the hippocampus and the amygdala, both of which play large roles in learning and memory. The hippocampus compares stimuli against existing memories, while the amygdala responds to emotional stimuli and strengthens associated long-term memories.'[4]

The more novel the experience, the stronger the memory. That's why we have strong, vivid memories of sleeping in a tent high up in the Himalayas a decade ago, but not so many about having tea with a colleague in the office cafeteria three weeks ago.

Relatability, Good and Bad Experiences

We have established that when opportunities for new experiences are presented to us, the brain scans for threats, especially physiological threats. Since the possibility of a tiger pouncing on us as we approach the intersection of two busy streets is limited these days, the brain takes on a new job—it scans for psychological threats. This is where relatability comes in. The human brain welcomes experiences that we can relate to—by eliminating those that are unfamiliar, the brain guides us through the day as a safety net, ensuring we stay within the limits of familiarity.

Think of a movie you like. Chances are that one of the characters reminds you of yourself. A picnic you enjoyed? It is likely you could relate to at least some of the people who were with you. Think of a team-building exercise at work that you remember with fondness. There might have been a few things present that you could relate to, or a few people you were familiar with. The converse is also probably true. People find it easier to say no to anything new that has no perceived element of familiarity in it.

Relatability draws people in, but novelty holds their attention. That's where curiosity kicks in. Despite our checks and balances, however, experiences are not always good. Maybe you landed up at a restaurant you never tried before because your friend asked you to come along (element of relatability), but hated the experience. Maybe the music was too loud or there were too many smokers.

Or the other time, when you went along for a trek with friends and the experience turned sour as it snowed heavily.

The brain remembers bad experiences better than good experiences, as established by several studies. Laura Carstensen, a psychology professor at Stanford University, says that in general, humans tend to *notice* the negative more than the positive.[5]

Some trace it back to our evolutionary roots, and indicate that this is a survival trait for humans. So, if a bear appeared out of nowhere in the middle of a trek on a beautiful trail, our brains will focus more on the bear than the beautiful mountains and the flowers in the backdrop.

And so, it reminds us that it is not advisable to leave any new initiative to chance. Experience designers are trained to map out experiences in a way such that every touchpoint in the experience journey is good, and the entire event leaves a positive and lasting impression on the mind.

Workplace Touchpoints

A workplace experience journey refers to traversing the various touchpoints of the organisation that a worker is attached to, irrespective of whether they are working from home or the office.

A touchpoint can be defined as, among other things, any way workers interact with the business organisation and the people in it, whether through a face-to-face meeting, doing focused work in the office, having online meetings from home or booking a seat through an employee app.

Organisational leaders are posed with the challenge of trying something new every now and then in order to improve the lives of their customers or their employees. At the same time, most recognise that introducing new corporate initiatives can lead to employee resistance, workflow disruptions and potential cultural clashes. The trick is to strike a balance between relatability and novelty. Brilliant new initiatives that have zero elements of relatability for the target group will often fail. Novel initiatives with elements of relatability will stick with the audience, as observers' brains are rewarded with dopamine.

Experience, understood as the process of living through an event or events, is what many organisations invest in these days. Earlier, experiences were designed only for customers, but there is now a growing movement towards creating experiences for employees to attract and retain talent.

In the day-to-day hustle to find the often-elusive work–life balance, it is, we believe, experiences that the modern worker's mind seeks, not things. Furthermore, experience must grow organically in the workplace. Good experience creators understand that one cannot simply manufacture experience. French philosopher and author Albert Camus said, 'You cannot create experience. You must undergo it.' Employers need to foster an environment to help their employees be prepared for novel experiences by developing trust.

A Post-Materialistic Life

There have been a number of adaptations of the 1964 novel *Charlie and the Chocolate Factory* by British author Roald Dahl. One of the most popular ones is a 2005 musical fantasy film by the same name, directed by Tim Burton and written by John August. In it, a young boy named Charlie, played by Freddie Highmore, lives in poverty with his family near a chocolate factory owned by Willy Wonka, played by Johnny Depp. Times are bad. Wonka's business is not doing well, and a lot of people, including Charlie's grandfather, lose their jobs. Charlie's father too loses his job in a toothpaste factory and the family struggles to make ends meet.[6]

To resurrect his business, Wonka announces a contest—golden tickets are placed in five random Wonka Chocolate Bars worldwide. Winners are promised a full tour of the factory as well as a lifetime supply of chocolate. Plus, one of the five winners is promised an additional bonus prize at the end of the tour. Charlie, with much difficulty, purchases three Wonka Bars and discovers a golden ticket inside the last one. He is overjoyed. When others hear about Charlie winning the golden ticket, he begins to receive very attractive monetary offers to sell the ticket. He considers trading it for money, as it has the potential to lift his family out of poverty. However, his grandfather gives him a pep talk and tells Charlie that he will have an unforgettable experience at the Wonka factory. After some initial reluctance, Charlie relents and decides to go on the tour, along with his grandfather.

Charlie's and his grandfather's decision to take a tour of the chocolate factory instead of accepting an offer to sell the ticket and get a roof over their heads that does not leak seems unrealistic. Who would not choose warm food and money? Those who are hungry, more often than not, are likely to choose money or food over experiences.

As individuals progress from poverty towards affluence, their needs change from physiological ones like food and shelter to those that are psychological. This concept has been theorised most famously by American psychologist Abraham Maslow and is now known as Maslow's 'Hierarchy of Needs'. It is a motivational theory in psychology that puts forward a five-tier model of human needs, often depicted as hierarchical levels within a pyramid. From the bottom of the hierarchy upwards, the needs are: physiological (food and clothing), safety (job security), love and belonging (friendship), esteem and self-actualisation.

SELF-ACTUALISATION
(Desire to become the most that one can be)

ESTEEM
(Respect, self-esteem, recognition, strength, freedom)

LOVE AND BELONGING
(Friendship, intimacy, family, sense of connection)

SAFETY NEEDS
(Personal security, employment, resources, health, property)

PHYSIOLOGICAL NEEDS
(Air, water, food, shelter, sleep, clothing, reproduction)

MASLOW'S HIERARCHY OF NEEDS

Needs lower in the hierarchy usually must be satisfied before individuals can attend to needs higher up.

Maslow's ideas have been criticised for their lack of scientific rigour. What holds true, though, is that as people, families, communities and societies move from poverty to affluence, their craving for experiences that add meaning to their lives increases, irrespective of whether they decide to invest in them or not.

With increasing affluence, people tend to replace their cars with more expensive ones, even though both fulfil their function of taking the rider from getting from point A to point B. Similarly, people upgrade from $200 smartphones to $1,200 smartphones as they move up the economic ladder, although the two devices may not be functionally very different. While the pricier model may flaunt a superior camera or higher storage, a significant portion of the premium is for the exclusive experience and social esteem linked to such purchases. The act of ownership fulfils a psychological need far more than any functional need.

Marketeers have understood this behaviour, devising strategies in which the product is only 25 per cent of the selling proposition. The remainder is an intangible feeling that is tied to the product, connected to how the product supposedly makes the customer's emotional life better. The story value that is sold along with the product is sometimes even more significant than the product itself. Stories, whether told or left unspoken, add real value to products because they are relatable.

But does the converse also hold true? Does every experience have to be associated with a product? No. For individuals accustomed to consumerism, where continual buying shapes identity and status, the significance of products and associated feelings may be heightened.

A section of the human population has spent decades chasing money and the experience of living a good life. As a result, they often focus on 'making money', mostly through hard work, making it the singular aim of their life. Hard work has allowed such people to buy bigger, shinier, sleeker things in the pursuit of product experiences that are expected to give them a good life.

The COVID-19 pandemic shattered this correlation between hard work, things bought with the money earned and happiness for a lot of people. In a way, it was the 'Great Awakening'. As the world got time to spend with their family, away from the office and the trappings of traditional work, the realisation dawned on many people that life is much more than wrapping oneself up around the singular idea of work. Many who can be considered financially secure began to view life from a different perspective. Instead of just more money, people wanted meaning—they wanted to experience things that added meaning to their lives, experiences that helped them become the best version of themselves.

Some people left polluted cities to live in the hills and breathe cleaner air. Many relocated from big cities to smaller towns to experience the joys of the outdoors. The direct financial consequence of this change in mindset was a drop in the premium for homes in urban centres in most cities with more than 1.5 million inhabitants, post-COVID.[7]

Many chose to work from home as it allowed them more time with their families. Millions quit their regular jobs, and for a lot of these people, the experience of living in a materialistic society held little meaning anymore. They had moved from the joys of owning things to the joys of non-materialistic experiences. In that sense, they had adopted a post-materialistic life, akin to a stage of self-actualisation.

Adopting a post-materialistic orientation is not new; it has always been available, even before the pandemic. Two things are new. First, the pandemic pushed many more to move in this direction. Second, the adoption of a less materialistic approach to life now appears to be happening far lower down the ladder of riches than it used to. For example, sabbaticals from work to pursue something that one truly loves or going on journeys of self-discovery were earlier seen as options limited to the Western world. Today, it is not surprising to see young people adopt such an orientation in many less-affluent parts of the developing Asia Pacific.

Millennials (those born between 1981 and 1996) and Gen Z (those born between 1996 and 2012) pick careers not out of desperation. They choose, instead, to align themselves with organisations that make them feel proud. They make more emotional decisions—sometimes not always purely rational ones— that add meaning to their lives. While such a post-materialistic orientation still requires them to focus on food, clothes and shelter as basic necessities, they refuse to look for the purely monetary gains in life and look for experiences that will be meaningful in a holistic way. This trend is paving the way for the emergence of experience societies, a topic we'll delve into in the upcoming chapter.

An Experience-Based Society

The Harvard Business Review, in an article in 1998, used the term 'Experience Economy' to explain how more and more people are spending their money on experiences instead of commodities.[8] One can define the experience economy as one in which goods and services are sold by emphasising their psychological effect and the joy they bring. But in reality, like goods and services, experiences have evolved into a distinct category of their own and can be sold.

A guided trek in the Himalayas is an experience that may be sold, and that is likely to be a mix of goods and services. So, when you go on that trek with your childhood buddies for one of your most memorable experiences, your total experience will be made up of, at the very least, an airplane ride, trekking, orientation lessons given by the trek guide and food.

When these goods and services work together, the resulting experience is perceived as far more valuable than the sum of the parts and becomes memorable.

Coexisting with an Experience Society

The experience economy coexists with an experience society. The pandemic disrupted consumption patterns as we knew them. The Amazons of the world entrenched themselves as a far more integral part of the human shopping experience than before. Netflix and their ilk entrenched themselves as significant avenues for the consumption of entertainment-related experiences. Similarly, the notion of work as a major part of the daily human grind shifted to an expectation of experiencing employment in a way that adds value and meaning to one's life.

Steven Miles, in his book *The Experience Society*, published in 2021, says we live in a world in which consumption is less about the 'using up' of products. Instead, it is an experience society, which is more about the maximisation of the moment. As we transition from meeting needs to consumption that addresses wants and desires, we are prone to move towards the consumption of experiences.[9]

In experience societies, people equate happiness with positive life events. Individuals who are creating an experience society choose meaningful engagement over just earning money. They dissociate experience and expenditure. Such people do not feel that experiences need to be exotic or in fancy, faraway places. They can be right where you are, a day working from the garden at home, a picnic with the family in a nearby park, a simple dinner with friends or a trip to the local farmers' market.

Gerhard Schulze, in the foreword to his book *Handbook on the Experience Economy*, mentions some characteristics of the experience society: deceleration instead of acceleration, less instead of more, uniqueness instead of standardisation, concentration instead of diversion and making instead of consuming. These attributes are not necessarily associated with material wealth.[10]

As more and more people subscribe to the idea of experience societies, the movement in this direction is gathering force. How can this movement be measured? Look around you. Travel and adventure tourism have grown significantly in recent years, with individuals prioritising unique destinations and immersive cultural encounters over traditional luxuries. On social media platforms, there's a notable shift from flaunting possessions to curating experiences, emphasising the desire for meaningful moments. People go on long weekend rides with friends, just to create reels or short, engaging videos set to music.

Businesses are adapting to this changing landscape, recognising the demand for experiential offerings. Immersive brand experiences, pop-up events and themed attractions are on the rise as companies seek to connect with consumers on a deeper, more emotional level. Subscription services, offering curated experiences delivered to one's doorstep, underscore the desire for ongoing novelty.

Moreover, the willingness to pay a premium for exclusive events or limited-access experiences, such as VIP concert tickets or personalised adventure packages, reflects a societal shift. People now value the intangible and memorable, demonstrating a departure from traditional consumerism.

Collectively, these behavioural shifts showcase the gathering force of the experience society movement. The way individuals spend, share and prioritise moments over possessions underscores a societal transformation towards embracing and celebrating the richness of lived experiences.

Millennials Leading the Change

The rise of on-demand services, propagated by the likes of Uber, Netflix and Airbnb, showed that this move was largely influenced by the younger lot, the millennials and Gen Z, who are quickly migrating to the experience society.

According to a study by the American event management and ticketing service Eventbrite titled *Millennials, Fuelling the Experience Economy*, 'More than three in four millennials (78 per cent) would choose to spend money on a desirable experience or events over buying something, and 55 per cent of millennials say they're spending more on events and live experiences than ever before.'[11] Some other key statistics from this report are as follows:

- 72 per cent say they would like to increase their spending on experiences rather than on physical things in the next

year, pointing to a move away from materialism and a
growing demand for real-life experiences.
- 69 per cent believe attending live events and experiences
  make them more connected to other people, the community
  and the world.
- FOMO, or a 'fear of missing out', drives the experiential
  appetite of millennials: nearly seven in ten (69 per cent)
  millennials experience FOMO. In a world where life
  experiences are broadcasted across social media, FOMO
  drives millennials to show up, share on social media and
  engage.

The generational shift towards prioritising experiences over
possessions isn't limited to millennials; it seamlessly extends to the
younger cohort, Gen Z. With an inherent desire for meaningful
encounters, Gen Z is actively shaping the landscape of the experience
economy. Much like their millennial counterparts, Gen Z exhibits
a pronounced inclination towards investing in experiences rather
than material goods.

The allure of live events, personalised encounters and shared
experiences holds particular resonance for Gen Z. They view these
moments as opportunities for genuine connection, both with peers
and the broader world. The desire to participate, document and
share experiences on digital platforms is a defining trait among Gen
Z. This tech-savvy generation actively seeks out real-life experiences
that not only provide enjoyment in the moment but also contribute
to their curated online narratives.

In 2014, Deloitte, a major global accounting firm, forecasted
that millennials would constitute around 75 per cent of the
workforce by 2025. While contemporary perspectives may differ
on the accuracy of this prediction, the current reality unmistakably

reflects a predominant presence of digital natives in offices, particularly with the integration of Gen Z into the workforce.[12] So, we are staring at a cross-generation of workers attuned to consuming experiences who go to the workplace with this mindset. For them, their professional life is not so much about a job as about what they do and how they do it. What are the particular manifestations of this on the work front?

Experience and Good Friendships

Most of us become friends with a few colleagues at work, and often continue to maintain such relationships long after we have left the organisation where we first met. Employees are often more loyal to their teams or to their friends at work than to the organisation that employs them. Employees often stay at an organisation because of friendships, because of co-workers they can relate to, people that they enjoy being with.

According to the *2021 Workplace Friendship & Happiness Survey* by Wildgoose, 57 per cent of people say having a best friend in the workplace makes work more enjoyable, 22 per cent feel more productive with friends and 21 per cent say friendship makes them more creative.[13]

In addition to enhancing job satisfaction and creativity, the impact of workplace friendships on productivity cannot be understated. Collaboration with people one likes or relates to fosters a positive and supportive environment. Research consistently shows that when employees share a strong rapport with their colleagues, there is a boost in morale and a greater willingness to collaborate effectively. When individuals enjoy working with their peers, communication flows more smoothly, leading to increased efficiency and a shared sense of purpose. This sense of camaraderie contributes significantly to a motivated and engaged workforce, ultimately translating into higher productivity levels. As the workplace evolves, recognising the value of these interpersonal connections not only promotes a healthier organisational culture but also serves as a driving force behind increased overall productivity and success.

Relatable experiences make people stick around. This brings to the fore the need to design workplace experiences that employees can relate to.

THE WORKPLACE EXPERIENCE

Experiencing Workplaces

Although most organisations are multi-generational, made up of Gen Z (born between 1995 and 2009), millennials or Gen Y (born between 1981 and 1994), Gen X (born between 1965 and 1980) and baby boomers (born between 1946 and 1964) working together, it is worthwhile to understand millennials' expectations of the workplace experience separately. This is not only because they have the largest representation but also because their and Gen Z's expectations from the post-COVID workplace are something that HR leaders are only beginning to fathom.

Many baby boomers were brought up with the idea of the American dream, whether they lived in the US or not. They push themselves to achieve their goals. This group has confidence in themselves and their capabilities. They have carved out a place for themselves, and they believe that working hard makes a difference. In contrast, the Gen X community is known for its independence. The first of the latchkey kids—children who are at home without adult supervision for some part of the day, as their parents are at work—they grew up more often with their mother in the workplace than the baby boomers. This ingrained a streak of independence in the entire generation.

Millennials do not see work as the be all and end all. Work, for them, is one of many things that define who they are. They want to experience work in a way that it adds meaning and purpose to their lives. Millennials and Gen Z are happy to walk away from work that adds no meaning or purpose.[14]

Fortune magazine did an article on the *Best Workplaces for Millennials™*. Along with a short introduction came a list, for 2022, of companies that helped millennials feel a sense of purpose as they work. For this article, *Fortune* partnered with the company Great Place to Work, which is seen as the global authority on workplace culture by corporate leaders. They help organisations quantify their culture and produce better business results by creating a high-trust work experience for all employees. Michael C. Bush, CEO of Great Place to Work, says this about millennials, 'How they spend their time and who they spend it with matters to them, as it should to all of us. Help them find meaning in their work. Give them a reason, many reasons, to be proud to work for you—and they'll stay working for you.' The *Fortune* magazine article further indicates that only 79 per cent of millennials say their work has special meaning, compared with 90 per cent of baby boomers. The article further states, 'When millennials believe their work has meaning—that it's more than "just a job"—they are three times more likely to stay.'[15]

Millennials come from a more experience-based orientation. They want experiences that add meaning to their lives and they may even care more about this than having a job that pays very well. Feeling a need for purposeful work is not something that is unique to millennials, however. It is true about other generations as well, including the baby boomers.

The statistics highlight a potential correlation between a sense of purpose in work and employee retention, indicating that organisations fostering a meaningful work environment are more likely to retain millennial talent. This insight underscores the importance of addressing and enhancing the intrinsic value of work for employees to positively impact their job satisfaction and tenure.

The statistics immediately below seem to indicate that there is much to be done by employer organisations. Millennials and Gen Z, especially, appear to be craving more personal meaning, development and purpose in the workplace.

What Ails?

'Millennials at work, Reshaping the workplace', a report by the consultancy PriceWaterhouse Coopers (PwC), highlights the following key findings. We paraphrase highlights from the report[16]:

Lack of loyalty: As much as 38 per cent of millennials who are currently part of the workforce said they were actively looking for a different role, while 43 per cent said they were open to offers. Only 18 per cent expect to stay with their current employer for the long term. A transient workforce may lead to recruitment challenges, emphasising the need for strategies that foster employee retention and satisfaction.

Work–life balance is more important than financial rewards: Millennials are committed to their personal learning and development and this remains their first-choice benefit from employers. In second place, they want flexible working hours. Cash bonuses come in at a surprising third place. As much as 28 per cent said that the work–life balance was worse than they had expected before joining. Employers need to adapt to changing preferences by offering meaningful learning opportunities and flexible schedules to attract and retain millennial employees.

A techno generation avoiding face time? With technology dominating every aspect of the lives of millennials, it's perhaps not surprising that 41 per cent said they prefer to communicate electronically at work than face-to-face or even over the telephone. Three-quarters of millennials believe that access to technology makes them more effective at work. However, technology is often a catalyst for intergenerational conflict in the workplace, and many millennials feel held back by rigid or outdated working styles. Bridging the technological generation gap is crucial for fostering effective communication and collaboration across different age groups in the workplace.

Generational tensions: Millennials say they are comfortable working with older generations and value mentors in particular. But there are signs of tensions, with 38 per cent saying that older senior management do not relate to younger workers, and 34 per cent saying that their personal drive was intimidating to other generations. Almost half felt that their managers did not always understand the way they use technology at work. Addressing intergenerational communication gaps and fostering mutual understanding is essential to create a harmonious and collaborative work environment.

These statistics paint a picture of a workplace grappling with a shifting landscape where traditional notions of loyalty, communication and management may not align with the expectations of the millennial workforce. The need for employers to reassess retention strategies, embrace technological integration seamlessly and bridge intergenerational gaps becomes evident. By understanding and addressing these concerns, organisations can cultivate a more adaptive and inclusive workplace, fostering loyalty and collaboration across diverse generations.

The Workplace in the Post-COVID Context

We have posited that the COVID pandemic has dramatically changed the way people work. Employees don't look at offices in the same way they did before the pandemic. And the word 'workplace' has a new meaning now. Office and workplace can often mean two different things, with the office often being a subset of the workplace.

Terms like workplace, workspace and office are sometimes used interchangeably and may cause confusion. For the sake of easy understanding, we thought it pertinent to mention upfront what we are referring to when we use these terms.

A **workspace** is a unit of physical space within which one works. This could be a traditional workstation, a cubicle, a focus pod, a meeting room, a phone booth, a tab, or any other space from which a worker can deliver work output individually or in a group.

An office or offices are where white-collar workers have traditionally gone to work.

A **workplace** is a combination of the office, home office, any remote workspace and the metaverse combined. All these different places are connected via technology.

Workers and employees get paid for working. We have used the word 'employee' as a generic subset of the word 'worker'. Workers include anyone who experiences workplace touchpoints within an organisation.

Knowledge workers are often referred to as white-collar workers. Knowledge workers are those whose jobs involve handling or using information. They are differentiated from other workers by their ability to solve particularly complex problems or to develop new products or services in their fields of expertise. They receive higher salaries that reflect the complex nature of their work, and their work is relatively independent in many cases.

The above are not definitions in the true sense but give an indication of what we are referring to in this book.

As a quick refresher, a **workplace experience journey** in today's context means traversing various touchpoints of an employee's organisation, irrespective of whether one is working from home or from the office. A touchpoint can be defined as any way workers interact with an organisation they work for, whether through a face-to-face meeting, doing focused work in the office, meeting online from home, booking a seat through an employee app, etc.

The challenges for organisations are first to understand the different workplace experience journeys that different categories of workers traverse as they represent many different generations; and second, to customise these journeys to meet the unique needs of each category and generation. Developing these understandings and customisations goes a long way towards expanding loyalty, improving the happiness quotient and increasing talent retention.

All is not hunky dory at work—not for the millennials and not for the others. Almost 90 per cent of executives in a 2021 study by Willis Towers Watson, a global solutions provider around employees, organizational risk and capital, said enhancing employee experience is a top priority. To put that in perspective, just about 50 per cent of leaders said the same prior to the pandemic.[17]

Work and the workplace need to be looked at through new lenses. What worked before may not work now. If talent needs to be attracted and retained, leaders across the world need to adapt to new realities. Amongst a plethora of things that leaders need to think through, the following three are crucial.

a) **Bringing back trust:** Trust suffered a bit of damage during the pandemic. It is critical to the employee experience, as without it, people won't stay on with their company. More than 55 per cent of employees left jobs because they didn't feel trusted, according to a 2022 survey by ResumeLab, which specialises in software to create beautiful, professional job application documents, including résumés. More than 60 per cent said the lack of trust at work affected their well-being.[18]

Trust helps create a positive employee experience. It is more important now than ever before to be transparent with information, to be personal with colleagues, to stick to commitments, to show appreciation, to listen to others and to demonstrate trust in them.

Conversely, many employees don't trust their employers. In a recent survey of 33,000 employees in 28 countries by Edelman Trust Barometer, it was found that one in three employees did not trust their employers. Edelman, a global communications firm, through the Trust Barometer, has been studying the influence of trust across society—government, media, business and NGOs—to shape conversation, drive results and earn action.[19]

b) Making it less blurry: The line between work and life blurred during the pandemic. Activities like virtual coffee breaks and happy hours emerged in the workplace experience journey to allow employees to relate to work in a new way during the worst of the lockdown.

In a 2023 change management project, one of your authors, serving as a consultant, engaged in interviews with leaders and facilitated focus groups with managers. These activities, along with others, aimed to grasp the organisational vision and assess the prevailing mood. In one such focus group workshop, an executive made a statement, 'Earlier it was a lot of travel, then it became no travel and only Zoom meetings. Now it's both travel and Zoom meetings at odd hours and places, leaving me with little time.'

Managers need to take a step back, and get rid of things that creep in on the personal time and interests of employees. For example, consider taking steps towards defining and putting in place habits and workstyles such that employees are not called in for meetings at certain times of the day or certain days of the week. At home or at work, if an employee logs in time for 'focus work', take steps towards keeping him or her free from 'collaboration work' during those hours, and so on.

c) Making things flexible: Flexibility is expected by almost all categories of employees. Within an organisation, employees seek flexibility about what they work on, how they work on it, when they work and from where they work. This essentially means redesigning work itself and providing a wide set of options from which employees can choose. This is quickly becoming a key tool for attracting and retaining talent.

However, offering flexibility is not a one-time initiative. It requires frequent interactions with different categories of employees to understand their changing expectations. It also requires policy tweaks. The trick is to stay relevant, which may mean investing in new technology, new working policies, new types of workspace options and updating the palette of workplace touchpoints that employees encounter every day.

There is an urgent need for organisations to adopt new policies and enhance their employee experience. A figure of 90 per cent of organisations making employee experience a priority, as quoted earlier, is a vocal indicator for the need to move towards a focus on continuously prioritising and enhancing the employee experience journey.

Enhance the Workplace Experience

We discussed earlier that the experience journey of employees involves a progression of organisational touchpoints. A touchpoint is any direct or indirect contact an employee has with the employing organisation. Throughout the workday, employees go on a journey encountering a variety of touchpoints. Employee touchpoints can be encountered within and outside an office. In a world where employees work virtually as well as from offices, touchpoints can vary from having lunch in the office cafeteria and having an online interaction over a digital platform to having a sandwich delivered to a meeting room via an employee app.

Enhancing the employee experience journey calls for an alignment of leadership goals and employee aspirations, supported by relevant technology. And in order for leaders to do this, it is imperative they understand employee aspirations in an ongoing manner, backed by data and analytics. All of this needs to be anchored around purpose and the meaning that employees seek from work. If this process is handled correctly, employees are empowered, specific business goals are more likely to be achieved and people outcomes are more easily met.

All these steps will contribute towards letting go of legacy mindsets, for it is time that the voice of the employees becomes louder and more pertinent than ever before.

Employees' Voices Matters

The move to an experience society and the radically changing world of work are not simply consequences of the COVID-19 pandemic. These changes were already happening in the pre-COVID era— they just moved a bit faster once the pandemic began.

But what really made the difference were two things:

a) Technology became available that enhanced the change. Some of the changes that we hear about now, like the home becoming an extended part of the workplace, could not have happened without technology changes. Zoom, a sustaining innovation, to use American academic and business consultant Clayton Christensen's terminology, was categorically different enough that millions moved toward video conferencing. Christensen developed the theory of 'disruptive innovation', with *The Economist* terming him 'the most influential management thinker of his time' soon after his 1997 book *The Innovator's Dilemma*.

Platforms like Zoom, along with others, allowed hybrid work to function smoothly. All of a sudden, hybrid workplaces were more efficient—a divide had been crossed. And there was no going back. The pandemic expedited change. Without it, the shift to hybrid work would have progressed at a slower pace due to organisational inertia, traditional work norms and a reluctance to deviate from established practices. The absence of a pressing need for remote work may have hindered the urgency for change.[20]

b) Knowledge workers showed that hybrid work was good enough. In the pre-pandemic era, only a small percentage of knowledge workers and organisations across the world were regularly working remotely and were familiar with the technology involved. Very few organisations had meaningfully deployed technology that brought about workplace and real estate efficiency. But the pandemic meant that nearly every organisation and every knowledge worker had to adapt to new realities. Once knowledge workers showed that their at-home work was almost as good, if not equal to, the work they did in the office, the cow was out of the barn.

Paradigmatic Upheaval

The permanence of hybrid work stems from its harmonisation of flexibility and productivity, which meets diverse employee needs. The pandemic forced an abrupt shift, revealing the viability of remote collaboration. Now, the genie is out of the bottle, and organisations recognise the benefits—improved work–life balance, talent retention and expanded talent pools. This transformative shift somewhat resembles a paradigm shift, challenging the traditional notion of fixed office routines.

A paradigm shift is a fundamental change in a society's view of how things work in the world. The shift from seeing the sun as the centre of the solar system, as compared to having Earth at the centre, is one example. Similarly, the heart was seen as the seat of thinking and feeling before the brain was recognised as having these functions.

Each of these changes in perspective is a paradigm shift.

While not a formal paradigm shift, the en masse move to hybrid work after the pandemic is a major and a sudden change. Embracing hybridity signals a departure from rigid structures, acknowledging the evolving dynamics of work and paving the way for a more adaptable, employee-centric future, resembling a significant shift in how we perceive and approach the workplace.

Major change often does not stop with one shift. In technology, the shift from mainframes to personal computers followed by the move to smartphones exemplifies ongoing evolution. Economic paradigms, such as the transition from industrial to information-based economies, showcase continual transformation. Each shift sets the stage for the next, illustrating that substantial change is a dynamic, iterative progression rather than a singular event. In later chapters, we will discuss how the next shift in hybrid work is likely to be played out in the metaverse. Many leaders are likely recognising and acknowledging the current and upcoming shifts. One notable outcome of this awareness is their newfound commitment to actively listening to the voices of their employees.

Listening

As sales dropped and markets eroded during the pandemic, organisations that could afford to do so held on to their employees. Bonding over virtual coffee and happy hours became necessary, as most managers suddenly had to grapple with the challenging reality of managing teams remotely. All generations of managers in human history have been trained to 'manage by sight'. Managing people remotely was almost completely new. The experience of this new reality resulted in experiments meant to keep teams together. Such efforts were clustered around the general theme of 'caring for our people'. Associated with all of this was a general need to listen to employees, a task that became much more imperative during the pandemic and was subsequently carried out much more than in the past.

Almost every client we worked with during the worst of the pandemic, and since, has gotten used to doing more regular employee surveys to gauge the changing aspirations and needs of employees. Many have adopted other methods to engage regularly with employees and to present the organisation and leadership as more humane. The voice of the employees is being heard. Things are not being 'done to them' without asking—or at least, this is the message that most organisations want to make known.

Using Data to Realign Work Practices

There are three stages to regularly collecting data on employee expectations and behaviours. First, many entities send out a 'your opinion matters' message, mostly through transparent and empathetic communication. This includes regular updates on company happenings, acknowledging individual contributions, fostering open dialogue, providing health and wellness support and creating a positive work environment that values well-being alongside professional growth.

The second part is the collection of data. The third involves analysing data to derive insights that help with realigning work and business. Insights come when patterns appear in the observations we make in the world. They help explain why something is happening the way it is, and usually lead to 'Aha!' moments. Action plans and strategies should only be created after insights are derived. While nearly every medium and large organisation collates employee data, there is very limited evidence to suggest that these organisations effectively collect knowledge from surveys and follow up with actions.

The true power of understanding employee data is through recognising how worker aspirations intersect with the work they have accomplished. Recognising whether the dreams of employees are being met in their work is a complex task. Reading the signs and then making the organisation employee-centric enables it to deliver experiences that are relatable, yet novel. Relatability draws people in, then novelty holds their attention. Alternatively, well-meaning initiatives that are not data-driven often face pushback.

New tools have emerged that help analyse small data collected through surveys. SurveyMonkey Genius uses artificial intelligence to analyse survey responses and provide insights. It can identify trends, correlations and statistical significance in the collected data. Qualtrics, known for its survey platform, includes Text iQ for analysing open-ended responses. It employs natural language processing to uncover themes, sentiments and key topics within the text. These and similar other tools make it easy to draw insights from surveys.

Similarly, big data, like those picked up by sensors and cameras, can be crunched more effectively than ever before with the help of powerful cloud computing. All of these tools help organisations understand employee aspirations and behaviours in real time. These tools help managers take timely action and curate personalised employee experiences. Latter chapters of this book cover this in more detail.

Listening to employees is good. But listening needs to be followed by action. Actions resonate with employees when they meet their aspirations. Without such action, employees often quit.

Welcome to the Great Resignation. This phenomenon is an indication that listening, while a good thing, will not usually work as a standalone strategy and tactic for workplace transformation.

The Great Resignation

Once the COVID-19 pandemic tapered down, record numbers of people left their jobs across the world. This is now known as the Great Resignation. In November 2021, 4.5 million workers left their jobs voluntarily in the United States, with 3 per cent of the workforce quitting their jobs each month. Never before had this happened. Quitting reached an 'all-time high', according to the US Bureau of Labor Statistics. Furthermore, 23 per cent of the workforce, when surveyed, expressed an interest in switching jobs in 2022. This phenomenon was seen in other parts of the world as well.[21, 22]

In the US and in European nations, factors like burnout at the workplace, low wages, lack of sound pension policies and unfair treatment by employers have been driving this trend, mostly amongst low- and mid-level workers. On the other side of the world, in developing nations such as India, the employee churn is much lower and mostly visible amongst mid- and senior-level executives. A growing number of individuals in these parts are opting to depart from large, established organisations, choosing instead to either join burgeoning start-ups or embark on entrepreneurial ventures of their own. Having financially secured themselves, this shift in career trajectory is rooted in the belief that such a transition is poised to offer them a heightened sense of independence, a broader array of choices and, notably, an increased allotment of time to spend with their families. This strategic realignment reflects a broader societal trend wherein professionals are prioritising autonomy and work–life balance in their pursuit of fulfilling and meaningful careers.

The overarching truth is that people are quitting because, in the post-COVID world of work, they are not getting what they want. Talent is scarce and HR managers have a huge task on hand to retain and attract talent. But what, in particular, do employees want?

What Are Employees Asking For?

In today's job markets, it is not easy to hire talent that meets an organisation's needs, nor is it easy to retain talent. Post COVID, the rules of the talent retention game became even more complex because people wanted to move and employees demanded more.

Talent Wants to Move

Thousands and thousands of young men and women in cities like Bengaluru, India, have been employed by large global organisations, headquartered in Western nations, for work that helps service their global customers at competitive prices, such as coding and customer support. A large majority of these unmarried, educated young men and women migrate to big cities from smaller towns in search of jobs. They often share rented apartments along with others of the same age group. They brave big-city traffic daily and mostly eat cafeteria food during the day and order from online delivery platforms at night. When the COVID-19 pandemic hit, almost all of these migrants returned to their hometowns to live with their families. Working from home allowed them greater flexibility. They spent time with family, ate home-cooked meals and enjoyed more space than they had in their crowded apartments. As the veil of the pandemic lifted, these young people found it difficult to move back to the congestion of big cities. There was little that was novel about going back to the metropolis. Nor was there much that felt relatable in returning to the office. Many employees did not want to be there.

Early attempts made by organisations to 'get them back' to the office were unsuccessful. This led HR teams to devise remote and hybrid working policies that allowed employees greater flexibility about where, how and when they wanted to work. There is little evidence that shows these policies were successful. Many of those who left the big cities did not return; instead, they resigned and joined competitors that allowed them to work remotely. There was new-found relatability in the flexibility of working hours and location for employees.

A comparable trend of relocating from towns and cities to areas where individuals can be in proximity to friends and family, or where they experience a sense of belonging, has manifested in various global regions. HR leaders and team managers have not succeeded in keeping such employees engaged and loyal to their organisations.

On 1 February 2022, all Goldman Sachs employees who worked in the New York headquarters were asked to return to the Manhattan office. According to *Fortune Magazine*, '...as of late morning on that Tuesday, only about 5,000 of Goldman's 10,000 HQ workers had shown up—despite having had over two weeks' notice, and in seeming defiance of Solomon's (the CEO's) pointed desire to get everyone back in the office as soon as safely possible'.[23]

David M. Solomon, unwavering in his conviction that in-person collaboration was essential for the firm's culture and success, witnessed Goldman Sachs gradually adapting by allowing flexibility in roles, implementing stricter COVID protocols and acknowledging the potential impracticality of a full return to pre-pandemic attendance levels. As of October 2023, Goldman Sachs' in-person attendance in New York City lingered 10–15 per cent below pre-pandemic levels, with varying employee sentiments towards the return to the office prompting an ongoing debate on hybrid work models and the ideal balance between in-person collaboration and remote flexibility within the company and across various industries.

'The views around work-from-home have completely changed,' said Stanford University economist Nicholas Bloom in an article on the NBC News website. Bloom is the co-director of the Productivity, Innovation and Entrepreneurship Program at the National Bureau of Economic Research. 'There is no stigma around working from home now.'[24]

The examples presented reveal a clear shift in employee preferences towards working from locations that offer comfort, relatability and autonomy. These insights underscore the paramount importance of accommodating employee preferences for a more engaged and loyal workforce in the evolving landscape of work.

Employees Demand More

Irrespective of whether employees work remotely or in office or in a hybrid fashion, they demand more from the employer now than they did before. The seismic shift brought about by the pandemic has empowered individuals to voice their needs and preferences more assertively. This increased vocalisation reflects a broader awareness of the evolving dynamics of work and a desire for employers to recognise and address the evolving needs of their workforce in a more holistic and inclusive manner.

Some of these demands are well-articulated and some are not, and they vary from country to country and city to city. Scanning the internet, one comes across a variety of surveys conducted post-COVID asking employees what they want. While the demand for more flexibility and hybrid working arrangements are commonly known and have been covered in earlier chapters, the following are a few other common expectations employees have from their workplace, in no particular order.

Good work–life balance. The expectation of work–life balance and well-being have risen in importance. Achieving work–life balance involves harmoniously prioritising both your professional and personal life. Employees expect balance between both areas of life, thereby promoting their physical, emotional, financial and mental well-being. Work–life balance doesn't necessarily mean dividing one's time evenly between one's work and personal life. It is about having the capacity to complete professional tasks and still having enough time and energy to enjoy family, friends and hobbies.

More holistic benefits. In the blended workplace, employees expect that the concept of well-being be expanded beyond financial and physical matters to include emotional, social, family and career wellness. There is a growing realisation that by providing benefits and perks that honour different facets of an employee's life, organisations are not providing a bonus or ancillary programme— they are simply meeting a basic set of needs. Soon, having a total package that caters to different facets of an employee's life will be required. Fine points within benefit packages also matter. Some that should be discussed are mental health assistance, support for physiotherapy, financial reimbursement for work-related equipment used at home and options to go beyond the legally mandated holidays, vacation days and related paid time off.

Play to one's strengths. Employees consider it important to find a role that lets them do what they do best. Before accepting any new or changed role, an employee expects a discussion to define their roles in ways that allow them to bring their whole self to work, both professionally and emotionally. They wish to know what the daily routine will be like, with whom they will work and what they will be expected to do. This stems from the need to find opportunities for what they see as meaningful career progression.

Positive workplace culture. Expressed in a variety of ways, employees have become vociferous about their expectations of a workplace culture that prioritises their well-being, offers support at all levels within the organisation and has policies in place that encourage respect, trust and empathy.

The contemporary job market witnesses a profound shift in employee expectations and the dynamics of work. Noteworthy is the amplified voice of employees, now more assertive about their needs, driven by an increased consciousness of their overall well-being. As we transition to the next chapter, it becomes apparent that organisations are grappling a bit with the challenge of aligning with these evolving demands. This transformation in the employer–employee dynamic prompts an examination of the strategies and initiatives adopted by employers to navigate this evolving landscape and cultivate a work environment that is adaptable, supportive and centred around the well-being of employees.

The Employers' Response

A choice between a good work–life balance and a fancy salary; a choice between being a good parent or a workaholic; a choice between different jobs; a choice between being an employee or an employer—these have opened up in the post-COVID world. Employees have realised that employers are more likely to relent now in giving them the freedom of choice at work than before. They have also realised that their sense of self-worth need not be wrapped around a singular concept called work.

Employers, on the other hand, have realised that if they do not listen to their employees and give them what they want, they are likely to see employees leaving them for others.

We have been involved in consulting assignments in medium and large organisations that helped navigate changes to new ways of working and of managing expectations. A few things stand out as positives when it comes to the responses of employers to employees' demands in the post-COVID world: listening and acting, giving employees more choices, creating new human resource policies that help employees make choices and going beyond policies.

Listening and Acting

Listening appears to be one of the pandemic's positive outcomes as most organisations have retained this practice in one form or the other, long after the pandemic tapered down. Employers now curate opportunities for employees to engage with one another and bond, encouraging them to be brand ambassadors far more than one saw in the pre-pandemic days.

Listening to employees on an ongoing basis gives the employer an opportunity to understand employee aspirations. Engaging with them and creating opportunities for employees at all levels to bond give leaders a sense of the pulse on the ground. Through this, smart managers derive valuable insights about employee motivations, from seeing things that are usually not covered in surveys and recognising trends, peaks and valleys in employee morale.

While such engagement opportunities do help with spreading the 'we care for you' message amongst employees, much greater value is obtained from gaining knowledge and acting upon it, benefitting both the employee and the employer.

Not all organisations can take advantage of the bonus of lessons from engagement opportunities, however. This happens due to a variety of reasons.

First is **a lack of trained personnel to find insights, create strategy and drive action.** Many organisations have excellent teams and systems set up to conceptualise and run employee engagement programmes. However, not many have the internal understanding of how to mine benefits from the responses and reactions resulting from such initiatives.

Next is **lack of leadership commitment beyond listening to employees.** At times, leaders are happy to take a short-term band-aid approach to smooth over a current need. Buying a few percentage points of employee goodwill by offering a bonus to a few employees to prevent them from quitting can make a difference. That said, short-term successes, at times, prevent leaders from working harder to uncover hidden truths.

A clash between employee aspirations and leadership vision may also occur. There are times when responses from employee surveys point to aspirations that appear to differ from the leadership's vision for the organisation. At such times, the findings may not be acted upon. Even if they are, the resulting action may be cosmetic in nature, with leadership pushing their own agenda over employee aspirations.

External consultants are sometimes hired to help align employee aspirations with leadership vision. This often leads to solutions and strategies that work for everyone, although not always. Human resource strategies in this regard, used in recent times, have centred around choice.

Giving Employees More Choices

As seen earlier, employees in progressive organisations are being given a wide choice of work options today. Choices include **location choice**, where employees are offered a choice of working from the base office or from a satellite office. **Working day choices** can be given, such that employees get to choose which days of the week they wish to work from an office and which days they would like to work from home or from another location.

Some organisations are even offering employees the option to choose their working hours. Such **work timing choices** are offered in the hope of creating even more work productivity by honouring the time of the day individual employees are most comfortable working.

Work setting choices give employees the choice to decide how they wish to work. They need not be tied to a desk all day. They can switch from one setting to another, depending on the type of work they are doing. For example, for individual-focused work, employees can work from focus pods; for less-focused work, they can work in social areas; for collaborative work, they can work alongside colleagues in a lounge or in a collab room.

Through **mobility choices**, the choice of different transport options in commuting to the office is being offered by many organisations. These could be a combination of company buses, monthly train passes and tie-ups and discounts with cab hailing app companies.

A wider **food choice** is being given to employees. Heathier options have been introduced to menus. Additionally, employee apps are beginning to see the integration of food ordering features.

Organisations are giving employees options to consider **job role changes** within their entities. These changes can be based on a myriad of variables, including their interests, skills and stage of life.

Recent times have also seen the emergence of a few organisations allowing their employees to have side hustles. Also called **moonlighting**, this allows employees to work elsewhere part-time while they continue to hold on to their primary job. Such initiatives have been prompted by the growth of the gig economy, where employees work on projects of their own liking, from a time and place of their own choice. This move has met with some criticism, as not all consider this to be either ethical or sustainable. It has the potential to create conflicts of interest and compromise an individual's commitment to their primary job. Additionally, there is the risk of competition and confidentiality breaches if employees take on secondary roles with direct competitors. It may not be sustainable in all cases because of the potential for burnout, as individuals juggle multiple commitments that can impact their overall well-being and potentially affecting their performance in both roles.

Creating New Human Resource Policies that Help Employees Make Choices

While it's raining choices for employees, the choices are not without boundaries. Organisations that introduced new choices for employees quickly realised that freedom without boundaries may derail business operations and work efficiency.

For example, many organisations announced that employees could work from home or from the office. But they introduced a caveat—one could work from home only up to a certain number of days in a week or in a month. So far so good. Both the employer and employees seemed happy; it looked like a win-win. It was then noticed that most offices were sparsely populated on Mondays and Fridays, while the days in the middle saw reasonable occupancy. This added a new dimension: how do you efficiently run and manage building services like air conditioning and power on days that see only 10 per cent occupancy? How do you optimise the expensive real estate on lean days? So, some employers introduced another rider to the 'choice of days' at work: that when one chose to work from office on certain days of the week, they would have to choose at least two or three continuous days, one of which needed to be a Monday or a Friday. This, they hoped, would help optimise their real estate footprint, as it would spread out the employee load a bit more evenly across five days of the week. There seems to be no end to the number of riders or combinations of riders one can add to such choices.

That said, putting too many riders into a policy can be cumbersome. Organisations that do so may greatly reduce the perceived value of the options they have created for employees. Employers walk a tightrope when it comes to defining choices. In the post-COVID era, creating and operating such policies is complex; one size does not fit all. There is no one right answer for every choice. Expect resistance and be ready for iterations. It may be an emotional rollercoaster, but hybrid work policies are a very good tool to attract and retain talent. The post-COVID employee sees the existence of such a policy as a huge benefit.

Going Beyond Policies

Policies formalise the structure of work and workplaces. They make sure that organisations function legally and help define the choices given to employees. However, a non-flexible policy may, at times, be limiting because organisations house multiple generations doing a variety of job functions for various teams. With individuals expressing a variety of preferences, complexities arise.

Flexible policies have worked well for many organisations. But even these may not be flexible enough. One may need, after enabling flexibility through a policy, to formulate a particular type of agreement that goes beyond policy. That second step is called a working agreement.

Jane Haskell, extension professor at the University of Maine, explains working agreements as follows: 'Working agreements are guidelines that define how groups want to work together, and what they want in the working environment and from each other to feel safe and free to learn, explore and discover.'[25]

A hybrid work policy, for example, can be rather generic. It can contain elements that may not account for future situations. For instance, a hybrid work policy might contain the type of language we discussed previously—including wording about working either a Monday or a Friday from the office during each non-vacation week. A working agreement might then soften the flexible hybrid policy by introducing the ability for individual teams, if everyone on the team is willing, to start later and work later each day, rather than the regular nine-to-five.

The problem is that not every team within an organisation or every individual within a team may love a policy and its associated flexibility agreements. Some individuals and teams may need a bit more flexibility still. And some individuals and teams may feel that new policy guidelines, as well as working agreements, bring angst and get upset. So, certain teams may need to agree to work in unforeseen new ways. This negotiation or workaround is often referred to as a working together arrangement. Such an arrangement may or may not be written down and seldom leads to a signed agreement between two parties.

Here are a few characteristics of such arrangements:

- They are developed with active participation by all team members;
- They determine how the team works together within the policy's framework;
- Such arrangements are a reflection of positive behaviours that are necessary for teamwork to be effective;
- The behaviours are described in simple and direct language;
- The number of clauses in such an agreement is limited;
- The best of these arrangements is easy to share with new members quickly;
- In team meetings, members are reminded about the arrangements.

Here are a few examples of what such arrangements may sound like:

- At times when flexibility leads to potential customer/client problems, these are the steps that will be taken: a, b, c...
- Over holidays and heavy vacation times, efforts will be made by teams to find resolution for competing needs. If a stalemate ensues, this process will be used: d, e, f...

Or they could be as simple as:

- We will encourage each other to participate in every discussion.

- We will begin and end on time.
- We will respond to requests over email within four hours.

Novelty Yes, But Where Is the Relatability?

Thanks to all the choices being given to employees, there is a lot of novelty at the workplace, so much so that some touchpoints along the employee workplace journey feel alien. The risk associated with non-relatable touchpoints is that it is easier for users to say no to change than to say yes.

Human resistance to change, even when beneficial, stems from the comfort of familiarity. Consequently, leaving change to chance is a precarious approach. Change management emerges as the linchpin, providing a structured framework to guide individuals through transitions. It involves proactive communication, engagement and strategic planning. By acknowledging the psychological resistance to change, change management ensures a smoother journey, fostering acceptance and aligning individuals with organisational evolution. In essence, it transforms uncertainty into a navigable path, maximising the positive impact of change on both individuals and the collective entity.

Change management takes centre stage when it comes to helping employees adapt to new ways of working. Processes have to be tailored for need. In a good change management process, there is experimentation and learning from setbacks. Few change management processes involve the exact same cookie cutter approaches to innovation.

Change Management

As highlighted in the previous section, some of the more popular choices being given to employees include those of location, working days, timing, work setting, mobility, food and job roles. New-age policies such as those on remote, hybrid or agile work help frame the dos and don'ts around these choices. As such policies are generic in nature, working together arrangements help make the execution of such choices a bit more personalised and relevant to individuals and teams. However good the choices, policies and these arrangements may be, HR leaders often see resistance from employees, who perceive the policies as being unfamiliar. One has to remember that the default setting in the human brain is to resist any change that it perceives as a threat.

Remember the part of the brain called the amygdala. It interprets change as a threat and releases hormones related to fear, fight and flight. The brain protects people from change. And so employees, when presented with new work practices, may resist. With people being hardwired to resist change, organisations have to work cleverly.

'Ten Reasons People Resist Change', written by Rosabeth Moss Kanter, appeared in the *Harvard Business Review* in 2012 but remains relevant today. Out of the ten reasons covered in the article, the following paraphrased reasons are most relevant to the post-COVID world.[26]

'I may lose control.' People get used to a certain rhythm when working. When that rhythm is threatened, they may experience a sense of loss of control over what was considered familiar territory. Employees' sense of self-determination is one of the first things to go when they see change being thrust upon them.

'Whoa, this is too sudden!' Changes brought about at work may be viewed as too sudden by employees. The sudden announcement of policies, with little or no time to get used to them, is usually met with resistance. In our day-to-day lives, when we have to take an immediate decision, saying no is easier than saying yes. Policies crafted without employee involvement that are then suddenly announced almost never work. Effective change management involves making hints about upcoming changes and slowly building familiarity with such transitions. Better still are changes that employees can craft themselves. When employees are deeply involved in changes, they own them.

'Everything is different now.' When 'return to work' campaigns were announced, a lot of people found it difficult to navigate the change as working from home had become an indispensable part of their life. Coming to office when one felt the need to do so might have been acceptable, but being mandated to report to office three–four days a week? An entirely different matter. The argument often heard was that the world is entirely different now, so it makes no sense to follow earlier practices and rules.

'Can I do it?' People often worry that they will not be competent when asked to change. Employees wonder whether they can show the best versions of themselves in a changed environment. An example of this was when, all of the sudden, millions of people were performing tasks remotely through new collaboration tools during COVID.

'I will have to work much more than before.' Many employees complain that with change, they have to work longer hours. Before the pandemic, there was segregation between the home and the office, but during the pandemic, the home became the workspace too. Now, employees are working in their offices, and then, when they get home, they are sitting in on video calls at odd hours. Not all newly drafted organisational policies have been able to arrest the spilling over of COVID-era habits into the new age.

Change Management as a Discipline

It is not possible for leaders to always make employees feel comfortable with change. However, they can minimise the discomfort associated with alterations. This comes with managing change.

Leaders can mandate change, but if they don't have a plan for how to implement, monitor and report on the success of change they are setting themselves up to fail. As someone famously said, 'If you fail to plan, you are planning to fail.' Those responsible for launching new ways of working must support employees moving through changes so that they successfully adapt to new ways of working.

An article by journalist Kelsey Miller in the Harvard Business School blog[27] lists five compelling steps in the change management process. We paraphrase below:

a) **Preparing the organisation for change:** Organisations must be prepared logistically, as well as culturally, to be successful. Leaders ought to help employees recognise and understand the need for change. Gaining this initial buy-in from employees is very helpful in removing friction and resistance at later stages.

b) **Crafting a vision and plan for change:** Once leaders have picked up some knowledge from employee interactions, a realistic plan needs to be designed. But, before that plan is launched and before most changes can be implemented, leaders have to prepare their organisation for change and then pre-wire the plan with managers. Please note, there is a difference between preparing a workforce for change and pre-wiring the change. The first is rather general. The second involves subtle steps that begin with putting the plan in place. Once a workforce is prepared for change and pre-wiring with certain key managers is complete, the actual plan can be unfurled. The plan must cover: goals that are to be achieved, how success of the plan will be defined, identification of teams and members responsible for the roll-out, as well as steps and actions to be taken. Despite best intentions, things do not always go as planned. So, a good plan should also account for the unforeseen and be agile.

c) **Implementing the changes:** A strong plan will make it easier to implement change. Once launched, change managers must focus on encouraging employees and making it easy for them to take the steps necessary to effect change. A change communication plan becomes integral during this stage. While a variety of means should be used to communicate with employees, the keys are to be prompt in communicating to remind employees that change is needed, and to avoid giving too much information or irrelevant information.

d) **Embedding changes:** Once the roll-out is completed, leaders must take steps to prevent employees from going back to old ways. At times, legacy processes are so ingrained in the system that employees may slide back to the old methods. Change managers must try to embed changes within the company's culture and practices, thereby making it difficult to backslide. New organisational structures, controls and reward systems have to be used to help change stick.

e) **Reviewing progress:** Completion does not necessarily mean success. One needs to review and benchmark against the success criteria set out in the beginning by utilising surveys, focus groups and observation studies.

A Focus on Relatability

At the heart of change management lies balance between novelty and relatability. Change is rejected when something is seen as too novel and not relatable. A good change management plan ensures that users are first drawn towards something new by the introduction of elements that users can relate to.

Let us look at an example to help illustrate these points. This example involves the introduction of unassigned seating after employees have lived with a fixed-seating legacy for many years. Fixed seating refers to dedicated work desks for employees. Unassigned seating requires employees to book a seat of choice in the office when they decide to work from the office on a particular day of the week. Workers can select a seat from a menu of available places that are free and not booked by other colleagues. However, a move from a fixed seating pattern to an unassigned seating approach can be difficult as the loss of ownership of one's desk is not easy to handle.

While introducing a move to unassigned seating, elements of familiarity may be introduced to build in the relatability factor. Such elements could include restricting the seat selection to the same section of the office that one is accustomed to. Similarly, relatability would come with the ability to book a seat next to team members. A third means would be to automate prompts, showing a colleague when close team members block dates and seats in the office.

The ability to relate to familiar elements in an otherwise foreign setting slowly encourages people to try new things. The novelty factor of the change then allows users to explore new processes and new experiences. In the above example, employees, over time, begin to enjoy the ability to work from different work settings.

They can still sit with their old friends if they so choose. They have a mechanical means to know when and where the friends will be in the office. But slowly, the realisation sinks in that their old workspace is no longer missed. In fact, many employees, through a series of discoveries, come to believe that a larger universe of working options is actually preferable. They begin to enjoy the flexibility of working in private when they need to sit alone and appreciate the flexibility of having a different space when they need to collaborate, even if they are no longer sitting near their old friends.

Making It Easy

While it may sound obvious, employees need to be highly motivated for change to be successful. Even if all the other elements are in place for a successful change management process but employees are demotivated and frustrated, change can often fail. If team leaders cannot motivate their team to adapt intuitively to new ways of working, performance may worsen. The quality of work of employees may suffer, and productivity may fall. Furthermore, unsuccessful change management may lead to the resignation of the best employees. Earlier poor behaviours may actually not only return to an organisation but can also show up worse than they were before.

How do you keep employees motivated? Let us recap:

- Give employees flexibility and choices at work.
- Introduce policies to define and govern the choices.
- Enable people who want to work together to do so. This makes work more relatable at a personal and team level.
- Make sure that change management initiatives use prompts and reminders.

- Give employees clues when big changes are coming and involve them in the process of change when possible.
- Drive motivation by doing the small things that make a difference to employees over the long term.

Are these change management tactics always enough to ensure success? Well, nothing can guarantee success. But being proactive goes a long way towards ensuring people adapt to new ways of working. Proactivity leads to an improvement in motivation. And motivated people make implementing and enforcing change a little easier.

To reiterate, employees find it easier to try new practices when they can relate to them. People find it easier to relate when they are familiar with some element of the change being made. Familiarity brings comfort.

All of this implies that we, as leaders, need to think long and hard about what is familiar to employees before we create change. As we do this, we have to remember that employees will try out new things when there is ease of use. Thus, as we consider familiarity, we should also be contemplating how employees thought about the old ways from an ease-of-use perspective. And we need to do this before we begin implementing change management processes.

Change roll-outs ought to be centred around the duality of introducing familiar elements and ensuring employees can perform actions with less effort than before. In other words, change management should connect to the past while also helping the organisation do its work in less time, while spending less money and exerting less physical activity. This is what making work easier is all about. Our experience working with change leaders has shown that a focus on making things easy is key to making change management work.

Let us build upon some of the comments we made in the introduction. These examples are from the world of consumers but also apply to the world of work. People began buying more on Amazon after the introduction of one-click ordering. People began streaming more on Netflix after the service began auto-playing episodes. People began preferring cabs over driving with the rise of app-based cab operators like Uber. People instinctively choose the easier option.

It is interesting to note that in each of the consumer examples just mentioned, technology plays an important role. Giving flexibility and choices to employees has largely relied on tech tools. This has led to an explosion of worktech options. Although it may not be considered as a universal definition, we use the term 'worktech' here as a short form of workplace technology. It can be broadly described as the suite of technology tools that allow workers to navigate work and the workplace appropriately. Apps encouraging energy savings in the office, tools and platforms allowing employees to collaborate and socialise online and the integration at work of third-party tools like app-based cab hailing services are part of the worktech industry. Everything that helps make life easier for employees and are better for the planet fit under the fast-expanding domain of worktech. Products that help employees be more effective, motivated and able are at the base of the worktech revolution.

Irrespective of what kind of app is being added to the workplace, such tools have to rely on the dual entities of familiarity and ease-of-use. They prompt you to take action that you can relate to or are familiar with, like suggesting food items that you chose in the past or suggesting a type of seat that the technology knows you are comfortable with. They also reduce the effort of performing the action.

Employees have always wanted choices and flexibility. But those feelings grew during the worst of the pandemic. Employers decided to give both greater flexibility and more choices to employees, to a great extent. Policies then came up to bind the delivery of choices and flexibility, with the focus on motivating people to follow what was written down. Policies were often perceived as constant reminders to adults to do things in certain ways. It was not easy for adults to accept repeated appeals, however well-meaning, by managers about how to do new things.

Since it has always been the case that it is easier to say no than to say yes to newness, many organisations have had to be very careful about how to introduce more change into the workplace milieu. Fortunately, tools and apps are making life simpler when new policies attached to hybrid work could have driven many employees crazy.

Similar to the swift embrace of platforms like Amazon and Uber, employees are now adopting worktech in a comparable manner. Just as we don't pay much attention to the 'how-to' instructions when downloading a new consumer-oriented mobile app, the adoption of worktech follows a similar pattern. The learning process for these new technologies is often intuitive, reflecting the seamless and user-friendly experiences that have become characteristic of consumer tech adoption. Moreover, there is an element of familiarity built into them. Employees typically download employee apps and swiftly agree to terms by clicking 'I do' without delving into agreements or reading manuals. These apps are intuitively designed for user-friendliness, allowing employees to navigate effortlessly without explicit instructions. For instance, an HR app may have a streamlined interface with self-explanatory icons, making it easy for employees to request leave, access policies and communicate with colleagues. The simplicity and intuitive nature of these apps contributes to a seamless user experience, reducing the need for extensive reading or guidance, and enabling employees to pick up and use them effortlessly.

Technology providers understand that we want to relate previous experiences to the learning of their new tools. They know we want to feel familiar very quickly with new technology. And the providers make it easy for us to learn and adopt new software and tools. Unlike traditional methods, these apps provide a dynamic platform for socialising change by incorporating updates, policies and communication channels. Employees, accustomed to the easy navigation of these tools, become more receptive to organisational changes communicated through such tech tools. This modern approach not only simplifies the change process but also enhances collaboration, ensuring a smoother transition and greater acceptance of new initiatives compared to traditional, less interactive communication methods.

What we see today in worktech is only the beginning of the journey towards curating personalised experiences for employees as they navigate the new age of work. Secondly, worktech is not limited to apps, but much more. It will only grow from here because it promises to make things easier for employees.

A DIFFERENT WORKPLACE JOURNEY

The Rise of Worktech

Rolling out change has traditionally involved employees receiving ample doses of motivational messages along with frequent prompts nudging people to accept change. Human resource departments lead many change management programmes, and while they play a prominent role in these processes, they are increasingly supported by electronic communications. One can observe the rise of worktech as an integral part of the change-delivery process, accompanied by algorithm-based automated interventions. This augurs well with a generation of young workers—that is, millennials and Gen Z— who would rather choose from multiple options in a worktech app than be subjected to change-related motivational talk. AI-driven worktech tools have the ability to decipher user behaviour and electronically deliver customised choices and flexibility options to users. Cleverly written algorithms in such tools can bring in ease of use and relatability, making change adoption smooth.

Let us look at the evolution of worktech.

Most decisions in organisations have to be justified financially. The two biggest costs in running an office-based organisation are the staff and the physical infrastructure. Both these costs are impacted when it comes to offering employees choices, as described in the previous chapters. Fortunately, these costs can be influenced.

Before we make suggestions about ways to control costs, it is important to note that costs can be broadly categorised under two headings:

a) Work inefficiency: Productivity is lost when employees either do the wrong thing or they do the right thing in the wrong way. In hybrid work, a lot of inefficiencies can creep in due to irregular work patterns.

b) Office infrastructure inefficiency: With employees working in places away from traditional offices and cubicles, time and money are lost as they don't always have the right tools with them. Moreover, employees are no longer glued to a workspace for eight hours every working day. In such a scenario, the office space may be inefficiently used.

Worktech is fast evolving to tackle issues around work and office infrastructure inefficiencies.

Integrating the Parts

Hybrid work is going through an evolution as we write. This is fuelling the evolution of worktech, and a need to integrate the various parts is slowly emerging to address inefficiencies. Early signs of integration are seen under three broad categories:

a) Integration of productivity tools, boosting work efficiency
b) Integration of the physical infrastructural elements, boosting infrastructure efficiency
c) Integration of productivity tools into the physical infrastructure.

Integration of Productivity Tools

We are referring to tools that allow people to collaborate and meet online, such as video-conferencing tools and the like, as productivity tools for knowledge workers. The suddenness of the pandemic and its associated challenges propelled organisations to accelerate their adoption of many new tools, allowing them to better navigate a world where all office employees worked remotely. In the world of hybrid work, the lack of integration between these tools as well as the physical infrastructure in the office required employees to log in and out of multiple platforms and devices. For example, throughout a day, an employee might have logged in to a video-conferencing tool like Zoom several times from their phone, and then logged in a few times from the video-conferencing system in meeting rooms. This was burdensome enough. But when entering calls through the rooms, one might have been required to enter some form of authentication. Since this authentication was not done automatically, workers needed special usernames and passwords, which often caused quite a hassle. Then the same employee might have been required to use another collaboration tool, like Slack, from their laptop or phone in a different space to collaborate with a remote team. This might have required yet another process of authentication. This inefficiency leads to a lot of time wasted.

If this type of complication continued throughout many months, leading to a diminished sense of productivity and effectiveness, an employee might have been ready to quit in frustration. And instead of finding fast ways to integrate many pieces of technology, organisations just kept adding new devices, platforms and physical spaces from which employees could work. Instead of getting simpler, the workplace experience journey became seemingly more complex as the number of organisational touchpoints went up significantly. Although the introduction of tools like mobile apps that remember employees' specific personal choices is a positive step, if they are not integrated seamlessly into other aspects of work, they might be perceived as just another tool to manage. In many organisations, efforts are now being made to integrate tools into fewer or a single platform to create a smoother employee experience.

While we don't have all the answers to integrating productivity-enhancing tools, we know that this topic is incredibly important. And the sooner users and providers can come together on ways to meet the needs of organisations and workers, the better.

Physical Infrastructure Integration

A need to integrate parts of the physical environment that facilitates work has also emerged. It does not end there. Not only do different elements of the physical infrastructure need to talk to each other, but handshakes also need to be built between those tools and productivity tools as well.

For example, if an employee books a focus pod in the office, the room needs to suit the user's needs. Based on past selections, the lighting can be automatically pre-set, driving familiarity for the user. If an employee decides to drive to work, the employee app can present not only the best route but also help him/her pick a parking spot closest to the seat already selected for the day. At lunch time, the employee's normal food choices might be pre-understood. The employee might receive computerised recommendations for food based on their health records or past choices. An employee can order ahead of time, and the cafeteria will have the food prepared based on options selected.

Similarly, an organisation's backend facilities dashboard allows the building administration team to track the infrastructure performance, parking and mobility patterns, drink preferences and office occupancy patterns. Such tracking happens in real time. Data collected helps the facilities team discover trends, and trend analysis can help organisations take corrective action around a variety of problems and issues. Moreover, optimising asset management and promoting sustainability through efficient resource allocation, informed decision-making and trend-driven strategies minimises waste and energy consumption, aligning with the commitment of organisations to reduce their ecological impact.

HR, FM and IT Integration

The integration described in the previous paragraphs necessitates that HR, facilities management (FM) and IT cooperate and move out of silos. Giving people choices is something that is usually led by HR. But HR representatives will often need to work with FM and IT staff to make those choices effective.

Bear in mind that the integration of IT systems that work at home and in the office requires a fair amount of sophistication. Earlier, we took the example of an employee who books a focus pod through an office computer. Let's assume for the moment that the worker then uses a smartphone-based employee app to make changes to the reservation. Such abilities involve technological integration. But they can also involve requirements that the three departments work together, at the very least, with regard to making employees aware of what is possible.

Working together like this requires the emergence of **workplace management** as a mainstream need in organisations. The discipline has evolved significantly in the years following COVID-19, mirroring the dynamic nature of modern work environments. Initially rooted in principles of scientific management, the focus was on optimising efficiency through task specialisation and time-motion studies. However, as organisations grow in complexity and recognise the importance of human factors, the discipline has expanded to include aspects of organisational behaviour, leadership and employee engagement. Today, workplace management encompasses a holistic approach that integrates strategic planning, team dynamics and employee well-being, reflecting a nuanced understanding of the intricate balance between people and productivity in the contemporary workplace. Workplace Evolutionaries or WE is a community of workplace professionals focused on advancing the field of corporate real estate and workplace management. Their website describes workplace management as a dynamic, emerging discipline that designs and delivers an organisation's unique workplace experience, aligning it to strategic drivers and business goals.

The examples cited earlier, like booking a focus pod or picking a parking spot, are rather basic, even though each of these steps requires sophisticated integration and the working together of the three groups mentioned. But they pale in relation to what needs to happen for the three departments to work cooperatively around projects that involve AI, Internet of Things (IoT) and big data.

A smooth integration of existing productivity tools and the physical infrastructure will deliver acceptable employee experiences. But even more so in the future, acceptable integration calls for the application and integration of AI and IoT in ways that capture the big data that is generated. The next chapter touches upon the practical realities of doing so. Before we go there, let us quickly describe AI, machine learning, IoT and big data.

Big Data

Big data refers to large, diverse sets of information that grow at ever-increasing rates. Big data is also known by high volume, high velocity and high variety. In other words, there is more of it, it comes more rapidly and it comes in more forms.

Organisations have a history of capturing transactional data on sales, profits and losses. But today, they track additional data from their operational environments. For example, many organisations collect web data about customer behaviour, such as page views, searches and the amount of time people stay on their website. Analysis of such data can enable organisations to change their prices, do customer segmentation and make targeted advertisements. Location data can also be very valuable. The GPS signals from smartphones, as well as Wi-Fi connection information, empower organisations by helping them know where their customers are located.

The analysis of such data is called big data analysis. The power of big data analysis is not just in what one particular source of data can tell us by itself. The value is in what it can tell us when data sets are combined. Analysis of such data is fundamentally different from conventional data analysis. There has been a shift in focus from descriptive analytics to predictive and prescriptive analytics.

The old-style descriptive analytics answers questions about:

- What happened in the past? This is mainly about reporting.
- What were the sales numbers in the third quarter last year?
- What were the employee occupancy levels in office over the last six months?

Big data's predictive analytics aims to answer questions around:

- What might happen next?
- What is the best offer for this client?
- How many employees are likely to be in the office on this coming Thursday?
- How many and which parking spots are likely to be used tomorrow?

On the other hand, prescriptive analytics tries to fathom:

- How do we deal with certain eventualities?
- How will you know across the thousands of offices you might control in a city, whether you will have enough energy for your generators to keep your offices heated in case of a blackout?

Artificial Intelligence (AI)

AI is a sub-field of computer science concerned with building smart machines capable of performing tasks that typically require human intelligence. Associated with this is the term 'machine learning' (ML). ML gives machines the ability to learn by themselves and improve their own performance—hence, they develop the ability to act intelligently.

There are two types of AI: General AI and Specialised or Narrow AI.

General AI is the theory and development of intelligence comparable to that of human intelligence. Perhaps, one day, General AI will go well beyond a human's general intelligence. The technology for General AI does not exist, yet. What does exist now is Specialised or Narrow AI. Here, machines perform only specific tasks and they do a far better or quicker job with these tasks than humans. Specialised AI governs technology that goes into things such as self-driving cars, personal assistants like Alexa or Siri, big data analysis, and applications like Google Translate and ChatGPT. Recently, there has been a surge in the popularity of generative AI, exemplified by models like ChatGPT and DALL-E. This branch of AI utilises algorithms to independently create novel content, including images, text or designs, drawing inspiration from patterns and data it has been trained on.

A lot of this is achieved through machine learning.

Machine Learning (ML)

In conventional computer programming, the only way to get a computer to do anything is to pre-program it with specific rules and commands. ML reverses this approach. ML uses the ability to program machines to learn by themselves and improve their own performance. The algorithms in these machines allow them to identify patterns in data and then predict similar patterns in new data. What is especially important, though, is that the machines can continuously improve the quality of the predictions they make over time.

Let us look at this from a human context. In the past, computer programs were written to help us solve complex problems, like mathematical questions. There was no ability, in the early years of computers, to recognise faces or objects. Then the internet came into our lives. This generated a large volume of consumer data from a variety of sources and with increased velocity. That is, the data was coming quickly. It was also the case that computers starting to recognise speech and remember faces.

ML is a way for computers to 'know things when they see them'. They do this by producing the rules for their operating systems by themselves. This is done through heavy-duty algorithms.

Statistical analysis and tonnes of data make up the other core ingredients of ML.

AI is all around us today; it unlocks our phones through face recognition and it also diagnoses some types of cancer. Although there has been much talk about AI for the last twenty years or so, it has made tremendous progress over the last five. This has happened mainly due to access to high levels of computing power becoming affordable and access to big data and analytical tools. Large data sets are combined with intelligent algorithms and iterative processing, leading to ML. AI software begins to learn automatically from patterns and features in data sets through ML.

Internet of Things (IoT)

IoT extends the power of the internet beyond desktops, laptops and smartphones to a whole range of other things, processes and environments.

Before smartphones, we had analogue mobile phones, which were not so smart. When the internet was connected to mobile phones, the smartphone was born. A whole new world opened up. Now the smartphone helps us read books, watch videos, do our banking and handle the remote-control apps that take care of our homes. Connecting things to the internet through IoT results in the same types of amazing benefits. What happens if this concept is extended and every other person-made object on the planet is connected to the internet? What if lights, locks, furniture, furnaces, ducts and doors in the office are connected to the internet? Imagine the possibilities. That, in essence, is what IoT is all about.

When a device is connected to the internet, it means that it can receive or send information, or perhaps even do both. This makes them smart. We are living in a world where billions of objects are sensing, communicating and sharing information, all interconnected over the internet. These interconnected objects are collecting data regularly. The analysis that grows out of this collected data is then used to develop tactics, strategies and action plans. The data is providing a plethora of intelligence for planning, management and decision-making. This is what is making driverless cars a reality and smart homes so very common today. So, why not smart offices?

Information is often collected and sent through sensors. These could be sensors that measure just about anything, which can be attached to or integrated with objects. This essentially means that any object can be turned into a sensing thing. For that matter, one can put sensors on birds and animals and track their movement. One can put them in soil to monitor moisture content, or in the ocean to monitor salinity, or on humans who can attach wearable devices and monitor different aspects of their health. You can even use sensors to measure the rate at which you can change the salinity of soil by adding water to it.

With real-time access to such data, real-time action becomes possible. So, if a sensor in the soil detects that the moisture content is low, it can activate the irrigation system to release water. Now, take that one notch higher. Let us say that the irrigation system is connected to the internet and it knows whether it's going to rain soon or not. The system can then account for a downpour to take an informed decision to release less water into the irrigation pipes.

The information collected about moisture in the soil can then be factored against future weather predictions, for instance, calculations of what the productivity the farmland may be with certain crops. The prices of fertiliser and pesticides can also be factored in. When all of these factors are being collected either through the IoT or other sources, a farm can be run very differently than has historically been the case.

If we were to simplify, there are two main ways IoT works.

People connecting to things: Examples of this include wearable devices like watches, sensors on shoes and smartphones sending and receiving information.

Things connecting to things: Incidences of this are navigation systems in cars that connect us to petrol pumps, emergency services and essentially everything else that is on the map and connected. We are also at the early stages of having one car being able to sense another vehicle, even if that other vehicle is behind a building.

You can expand these definitions to include other objects and segments of society. Within those categories are smart offices, smart homes, smart cities, smart energy, smart education, smart factories and smart government. There are so many possibilities.

Uneasy Workplace Journey

AI, IoT and big data facilitate the integration of employee tech platforms with physical infrastructure. This integration, when done correctly, helps bring about a superior, relatable and customised workplace experience. For this to happen effectively, the HR, FM and IT teams have to work together under the banner of workplace management. Analogous to this is the wide variety of professionals working together to design, deliver and drive trips to outer space.

Space travel utilises AI, IoT, big data and cloud computing to navigate space. Cloud computing involves the use of servers, storage, databases, networks, software, analytics and intelligence—over the internet ('the cloud'). A mixture of telescopes, sensors, software, radar, GPS, laser beams and cameras can monitor conditions in space. One can well imagine how well-integrated different parts of a space operation have to be. Similarly, improving the workplace experience journey should be possible, now that all the technology is available.

If NASA can help astronauts navigate space, then HR, FM and IT departments ought to be able to help employees navigate the workplace better.

Integration in its Infancy

Even though all the tech needed is available, many organisations are unable to provide a superior workplace experience. The various parts of the technological and cultural puzzle are not fully integrated. This is partly because different tech and equipment suppliers have their own vision of how the future will play out, and at this point there is not enough interoperability for fluid integration.

Interoperability involves the application of two or more computer systems working together. A good interoperable system allows, for example, an online business to accept monies through PayPal. Or one could, theoretically, be able to send a message from a WhatsApp account to an iMessage user. Unfortunately, however, Facebook and Apple, the owners of these means of communication, do not allow us to communicate in this way.

Sophisticated software is also used in a Tesla autonomous vehicle. Good interoperability will mean that Tesla's governance system can effect a flawless handshake with the governance system of another autonomous vehicle manufacturer to make road travel safe. Imagine this—as a Tesla vehicle approaches an intersection, its software senses an approaching vehicle and communicates with the governance system of the other vehicle well ahead of the intersection and slows down or stops the car, as required.

Since equipment suppliers protect their turf, we are not anywhere close to a smooth integration between various physical components that go into office infrastructure, such as lights, air conditioning, energy, etc. Similarly, we are also not close to a smooth integration between all the software systems behind these equipment and third-party apps. Technology is not open, and integration is still a work in progress today. Most organisations rely on multiple productivity platforms to get various aspects of their work done, although attempts are being made to integrate. It is a bit of a struggle for knowledge workers as they navigate a workplace that blends the physical and the virtual worlds, jumping from one platform to the other. Although the flexibility of working from home sounds exciting, it is not easy to adjust to consistent change. The workplace journey, with multiple touchpoints, is not yet smooth.

Shaking Off COVID-Infused Practices

When many white-collar workers were forced to work remotely during the COVID lockdown, a quick adoption of productivity and collaboration tools was required to keep the wheels of business running. Virtual coffee meets replaced catch-ups in the office cafeteria. Virtual water cooler moments became common. Virtual team-building exercises were introduced. All types of meetings and interactions went online. Platforms like MS Teams and Zoom, that existed in the pre-COVID era, were improved upon, and employees began using them for many more types of interaction. The platforms continued to innovate and allowed for more and more different types of interaction to happen. For example, Microsoft Teams introduced the Bookings app that lets businesses quickly and easily schedule, manage and conduct virtual appointments. Then they added the Tasks app that replaced the existing Planner app and allowed users to organise everything in one place as well as quickly schedule and assign tasks to team members.

Some of the COVID-era traits and problems remained after employees began returning to work. The default setting had changed. A very short example may demonstrate one of these bad habits, even though it is very particular. Unfortunately, other problems of equal importance developed as well.

Our example is about how workers attended ideation sessions with cameras off. This is akin to attending a creativity session with blinders on. Creativity and ideation stem from the periphery, from responding to all five senses. Creativity and ideation are not linear processes. Non-verbal cues, such as body language and facial expressions, play a crucial role in communication and understanding, enhancing the depth of brainstorming sessions. While virtual sessions offer convenience, in-person interactions often tap into the essence of human connection, creating a conducive environment for innovation and creative breakthroughs.

Alternatively, a different meeting may require another approach. An online presentation to a thousand employees about the quarter's results may not warrant having everyone show their face on camera. But a four-person brainstorming session would feel a little lonely, as if the participants are speaking into the ether, if the cameras are off.

All managers should be trained to deliver the same experience to remote workers that they provide to their in-office colleagues. The overall experience of work, irrespective of one's location, ought to be uniform. Without such equality, the hybrid work model will erode. If at-home workers recognise that they are being denied the professional success enjoyed by in-office colleagues, they will end up making a choice—either they stay with their employer and accept fewer promotions and smaller raises, or they speak up and make their feelings known. The third option is that they leave their employer.

Our feeling is that there are some industries in which employers simply must accept that employees are going to demand equal treatment for at-home work. These employers will have to address some valid concerns from younger workers such as mentorship. If many older, more experienced employees are working from home, they will not be able to provide the type of in-person, informal mentorship that was so often given when everyone worked from the office. A partial answer to this problem is the hybrid office.

Things Are Changing

In 2022, Microsoft announced the launch of Microsoft Places as an add-on to the Microsoft 365 platform. Their goal was to 'optimise the use of physical space'. Places provides insights into when workers are coming into offices and which meeting times are best suited for an in-person versus remote set-up. The following paragraph from a blog post by Jared Spataro, Corporate Vice President for Microsoft 365, announcing the launch of Places, highlights the need to integrate physical and digital spaces in a world of hybrid work:[28] 'Microsoft Places' hybrid scheduling will leverage common data signals from Outlook and Teams to allow you to view the week ahead and see when your co-workers and close collaborators are planning to be in the office. You'll understand the days with the most in-office attendance, allowing you to adjust your schedule to take advantage of valuable in-person connections. Intelligent booking will help you discover available spaces with the right technology to match your meeting purpose and mix of in-person or remote participants. And you'll get recommendations for the shortest commute times – with prompts telling you when to leave based on that day's traffic and when your meetings are scheduled. With Microsoft Places, you can prioritize your time while maximizing in-person connections.'

This launch is a welcome move, but the company will continue to upgrade the product. This will happen based partly on Microsoft's own vision of how the future will play out and partly to protect their turf. Our guesstimate is that it will be integrated with Microsoft 365, which is a suite of comprehensive office-related services. A comparable product is Google Workspace.

Microsoft Places could integrate with some components of the physical office and with some suppliers of components such as lighting and air conditioning. The platforms of their competitors could integrate with other suppliers of such components. The possible lack of interoperability between the two systems, due to different platforms protecting their turf, would make it difficult for workplace management stakeholders to easily design and deliver consistent employee workplace experiences. This opens up the opportunity for niche players, like Freespace, that deliver customised integrated solutions to clients, based on the organisation's choice of physical components and productivity tools.

The launch of generic solutions like Microsoft Places and customised offerings by players like Freespace begins a journey headed towards a transition to employees working in the metaverse in the not-too-distant future.

Future of Worktech and the Metaverse

Parts of worktech today are poised to transition to the metaverse in coming years. The integration of work productivity platforms with physical infrastructure is just the beginning. The world of work is hurtling headlong towards a base on the metaverse. A fascinating convergence unfolds as the metaverse grows alongside increased demands for fair employee benefits and reducing discrimination against remote workers.

There is no singular definition of the metaverse. The word first appeared in 1992, when science fiction writer Neal Stephenson wrote about the concept in his book *Snow Crash*. The concept found its way into Hollywood movies like *The Matrix*, but it was not until 2021, when Facebook rechristened itself as Meta, that the word quickly gained popularity. In the announcement about the name change, Meta said it sees itself evolving into a metaverse company by 2027. After Meta's announcement, other tech giants were quick to state their intentions of setting up their own versions of the metaverse.

Broadly speaking, the metaverse is a persistent, online, 3D universe that combines multiple different virtual spaces. In other words, it is a 3D internet. It allows users to work, meet, socialise and play games with other users in these 3D spaces.

As it stands, the metaverse does not yet exist as per our definition. But some platforms offer early versions of metaverse-like elements. For instance, virtual reality games give us a peek into what the metaverse may be like. They offer a place where one can buy virtual real estate, virtual attire for avatars and virtual personalities, among others, setting the stage for virtual economies.

Let us be clear from the onset. We are not excited about all the elements of what is to come. That said, organisational leaders should be prepared. Not having a plan leaves open the option of the unfavourable side of metaverses becoming the norm, with blurred lines between personal and professional life, isolation and addiction emerging out of overreliance, heightened cyber threats and the like.

The summary of a market report from the website of Fortune Business Insights says: 'The global metaverse market size was valued at USD 63.83 billion in 2021. The market is projected to grow from USD 100.27 billion in 2022 to USD 1,527.55 billion by 2029, exhibiting a CAGR of 47.6% during the forecast period.' This growth is largely due to the accelerated demand for online gaming and shopping. Significant investment is being made in these areas—for example, Nike, the apparel and shoe brand, collaborated with gaming company Roblox Corporation to create a virtual world called Nikeland in 2021. Nikeland enables avatars to dress up in Nike's branded apparel and sneakers. The same report further mentions that, in 2021, Epic Games received $1 billion in funding to support future opportunities in the metaverse growth market.[29]

Future areas into which the metaverse can develop include social media and the world of work. As societies get used to alternative realities through gaming and shopping, there will soon be demand for metaverses on social media platforms. For these platforms, one of the key benefits of the metaverse is the potential to personalise one's digital identity. In traditional social media, there is often pressure to conform to certain beauty standards, leading to body image and self-esteem issues. In the metaverse, users can create avatars that represent them in a more abstract or imaginative way, reducing the emphasis on physical appearance.

A similar demand may arise from employees, likely driven by a desire to, for instance, turn off their cameras for virtual meetings and use an avatar instead. The growth of hybrid work will aid the growth of the metaverse as employees seek to not show their faces in every video conference. Moreover, the metaverse could provide a more inclusive and accessible space for people with certain disabilities. Virtual environments can be designed to accommodate various needs, offering a more level playing field for social and work-related interactions.

Although the tech giants appear to be leading the metaverse movement, many decentralised aspects of the metaverse allow smaller players to participate in its development. Projects like Decentraland and Cryptovoxels leverage blockchain for user-owned virtual spaces and assets. On the other hand, initiatives like Interledger Protocol and Cosmos focus on creating interoperability standards for seamless communication between various metaverse components. The real game changer will come as giant tech companies enable work to be carried out in big ways in a metaverse or multiple metaverses. The realisation of such a concept will also mean that virtual economies will be created, where cryptocurrencies, often provided by smaller players, may play an important role. The confluence of financial, physical and virtual worlds is the future, as bothersome as the thought may be.

We know the metaverse is coming. We do not know how fast the most impactful aspects will become a reality. We know that there will be many beneficial aspects to them. And we also know there will be some real downsides. All three of your authors do not dismiss these. While there are others with far gloomier fears, we worry about certain outcomes. Imagine a young person so convinced that a version of the metaverse is so real that he/she never goes outside. Never feels the sun shining directly onto their skin. Never swings on a real tree swing. Never gets their feet wet crossing a stream. Our fear is that the metaverse will be so appealing on some levels that scenarios like this may actually play out. Of course, everyone deserves the right to stay inside. But if a significant percentage of human beings made this choice, there could be ramifications for the rest of us that are hard to calculate. But mostly, we are concerned for some introverts who believe that real community can only be built for them through avatars that cannot experience life as we know it.

Hybrid Work Fuelling the Need for the Metaverse

Many of the workplace journeys today are made complex by the lack of smooth integrations between different platforms, the lack of alignment between tasks and the appropriate work setting and the lack of equality between the in-office and remote experience. Employers and employees will gravitate towards the metaverse because of two other reasons, which serve to offset these negative aspects. First, the metaverse will provide a smooth integration of workspaces at the office and the home. Second, it will be significantly used by a certain percentage of companies. Then, as so often happens, once a trend is established, everyone who can will join in.

We have just made a bold projection. And we do this at a time when no standard for hybrid work has emerged for organisations to follow. However, with the pros of adopting a hybrid work model seemingly outweighing the cons, hybrid work is likely to stay.[30] For one, it is one of the most preferred choices amongst knowledge workers today. And, in the current hunt for scarce talent, one of the biggest advantages a company can grant its employees is the ability to work from home. Data scientists at the US-based career site Ladders projected in December 2021 that remote opportunities will continue to increase through the years. Remote opportunities leapt from being under 4 per cent of all high-paying jobs before the pandemic to about 9 per cent at the end of 2020, and to more than 15 per cent towards the end of the pandemic's worst moments.[31] Such trends also mean that organisations now have diverse workers being employed on a remote basis, including full-time workers, part-time workers, contractual workers and temporary workers.

The metaverse will exist partly because change grows out of challenges to existing paradigms. With many different workers negotiating choices about when, how and where they work, old paradigms are disintegrating. It is not clear what the details of the new meta paradigm will be, but it is clear that change is coming and it will be forward-looking.

Let us now backpedal a little. There are reasons that the old paradigm will survive, at least for a few years. In the country where two of us live, England, the economy shrunk by 0.5 per cent in July 2023. If prognosticators are right and recession hits much of the Western world for a prolonged period, employees may be less likely to ask to work from home. Proximity bias is at the root of fears of employees who work from home. It is predicated on the assumption that workers who interact regularly with colleagues and bosses in the office will get ahead, while those who work remotely regularly may lag behind. This is an apprehension, but if workers recognise a link between being in the office and their professional success, and they feel that recession will lead to some workers being terminated, then many may choose to work regularly from offices. This may then damage the hybrid work model and upset some of the metaverse assumptions we have stated.

Individual leaders may have difficulty in managing hybrid teams, but many organisations want the hybrid model to work. It brings tremendous cost efficiencies, it helps the carbon footprint agenda and allows access to a dispersed talent pool from anywhere in the world. These three factors are likely to push the hybrid work movement forward, despite any initial roadblocks that leaders are likely to face or any bouts of recession that may come.

While we believe that hybrid work is here to stay, organisations must, nonetheless, strive to remove proximity biases against hybrid work. Toward this end, effort must be made to allow a uniform overall experience for workers, irrespective of whether they work remotely or from the office. The metaverse may be a unifying factor in this regard. Once a remote worker is onboarded onto the organisational metaverse, he or she could receive access to the same digital work environment as office workers.

Tech giants see an opportunity here and have fuelled the narrative of the metaverse being the solution to the remote vs office worker divide. Meta imagines the metaverse as a unification of physical and virtual realities enabling peer-to-peer, life-like interaction in digital work environments. Such a unification of the physical and the virtual is also often referred to as augmented reality by others. Others imagine the metaverse as a parallel universe that humans will inhabit for work and for recreation. Although different tech giants may have slightly different visions of how the metaverse will play out, what appears to be a common understanding is that irrespective of a worker's location, it is the metaverse that will give workers a homogeneous experience.

Learnings from Other Platforms

The metaverse is being built on learnings gleaned from the success of digital platforms that use AI and big data to deliver relatable content and dopamine fixes to users. Social media platforms, networking platforms, e-commerce platforms and online streaming platforms are examples of this. Two key characteristics that stand out are:

Relatable content: Algorithms track our online behaviour to create a digital impression of our likes and dislikes. Based on such individual profiling, a variety of relatable content is pushed our way. The range of content consumed within the boundaries of our likes widens, and we get hooked. The relatability draws us in, and the novelty of new content makes us stick.

Dopamine generation: Getting hooked to these platforms and the content generated within serves us our daily dose of dopamine. Often, navigating such platforms requires no effort.

Picking from these and other learnings, development teams are striving to make the metaverse effortless for users, with ease of use being one of the main drivers. The metaverse is pulling humanity in a direction where work may no longer feel like work, especially for knowledge workers. This is where the concept of making work easier makes its entrance.

A Day in the Metaverse

So, what will a typical workday in the metaverse look like as compared to work today? Today, we use our smartphones to conduct many of the most important aspects of our day-to-day lives. Everything is just a click away. One of the first things most of us do in the morning is to look at our phone. We see who has written to us. We look at what we have scheduled for the day. We use our phones to check the weather. Throughout the day, the smartphone or our computer is our digital assistant; one or the other of the two often pings us, guiding us to complete the next thing on our to-do list. This role of a digital assistant is personalised to our individual tastes, and it serves to make our lives easier. In the metaverse, it is likely that this role of the smartphone will be replaced by augmented reality, or AR, glasses. AR glasses could potentially become the window to the world for many.

A made-up story may help illustrate what we believe may unfold. So, let's say Mike, in the not-so-distant future, is woken up by an alarm from his AR glasses kept by the bedside. These cool glasses are likely to look very similar to your average reading glasses but will be able to do much more. As Mike gets up from bed, he puts on the glasses. The glasses scan Mike's iris, detect that he is awake and, through their built-in speakers, say something like this: 'Good morning, Mike. It is a rather wet Tuesday today, and you have three meetings lined up. Do remember to carry your umbrella. Do you want to know which are those three meetings?'

As the glasses connect to the cloud and help prepare Mike for the day, they also begin to tap into Mike's biology. The glasses record his body temperature and send it to his organisation's cloud so that he gets all the clearances automatically to be in the office that day. On a day when Mike's vitals are a bit off, his AR glasses may ask him, 'Hey Mike, you are running a body temperature of 101 degrees. May I recommend that you visit your doctor. Would you like me to set up an appointment with Dr Roberts?'

Mike finishes his breakfast, and the glasses remind him to take his prescription medicine. As he heads towards the closet to get ready for work and stands in front of the mirror, his AR glasses help him go through a variety of outfit options. In the mirror, he can see himself trying out various outfits. As he has two very formal meetings, the glasses show him only those outfits that will be suitable for these meetings, guiding him with a variety of tips along the way.

There are days during the week when Mike works from home. In meetings on those days, an avatar of Mike is projected in the office boardroom—such hybrid meetings have a mix of people in person and appearing as avatars online. When Mike decides to attend meetings like this, his glasses help him pick the attire that the avatar should wear that day. Mike uses cryptocurrencies to buy digital attire from popular retailers of formal and informal wear. As he sits at his desk and continues to use his AR glasses, his office at home is transformed into a boardroom and he can interact fully with other members in the meeting.

Mike gets ready to leave for the office, a fifteen-minute drive away; his AR glasses look for the most appropriate share cab from the ride-sharing service affiliated with his organisation. The glasses help Mike synchronise his walk to the pick-up point with the cab's movement and he boards it without having to wait for more than a minute. Mike's smartwatch counts his steps, and he periodically gets the updates on the visor of his glasses. Mike's vital health statistics are also constantly updated with his health insurance company and his premiums are adjusted on the basis of his health status.

On days when Mike decides to drive to work, his glasses help him find a parking spot in his office's parking lot and guide him to it.

As Mike enters the office premises, the doors in front of him open as a facial recognition algorithm grants him access. Depending on the various tasks lined up for the day, Mike's glasses guide him through the day. His glasses book meeting rooms and other workspaces for him. As he walks from one part of the office to the other, the building services respond based on his movements. Lights and air conditioning turn on as he enters a room and shut down as the room is vacated. Occupancy sensors send signals to the building management system (BMS), which in turn records his preferences for the future. Thirty minutes before lunch time, Mike's AR glasses ask him if he would like to order some food. Based on his previous picks, his doctor's prescriptions, his current health parameters and food choices available, Mike is given the most appropriate options from which to select. The glasses also allow Mike the opportunity to choose a few colleagues he may want to have lunch with, based on his past behaviours.

Mike orders a sandwich, the payment for which is confirmed with the AR glasses scanning his iris. A digital receipt is shown and then placed in an expense tracker, reminding Mike how much he has spent on lunch so far this month. As the payment is completed, Mike is also asked if he would like to buy a gift for his boss's anniversary, which is in two days. A few gifting options are suggested, based on the algorithm's understanding of his boss's likes and dislikes. He postpones that decision for later.

Mike gets an alert as his lunch arrives and he sits down to eat with Joanna. Mid-way through lunch, he gets a call from his boss, whose hologram appears next to Mike at the lunch table.

'Hey Mike, can I catch you for a few minutes after you have finished lunch?' asks his boss.

'Sure, boss, please give me about fifteen minutes,' Mike says, and the hologram disappears.

As employees in Mike's office do not have assigned seats, Mike's AR glasses find his boss's exact location and guide him through the wayfinding mode to the lounge where his boss is seated.

'Hey Mike, I wanted your opinion on the new explainer that the agency has sent.'

Their metaverse social marketing agency has sent across an iteration of an immersive explainer video. Mike's boss plays the video, and suddenly a virtual girl appears as a holographic projection and guides them into a virtual realm that showcases their products. The girl, called Ruth, speaks to Mike in a personalised tone, drawing from the information the algorithm has gathered from the organisational cloud about Mike.

'This looks good, boss. My only concern is that Ruth has been designed to be too perfect—she looks like a model. We should make her a bit more realistic...just to make the explainer seem real.'

'Hmm, you're right...I thought so too. Thanks, Mike. I will ask them to make the changes and send us the updated explainer,' Mike's boss responds.

Later, during a team meeting in the afternoon, the interior designer assigned to put together a new office plan makes a presentation to Mike and a bunch of his colleagues, some of whom join in remotely, with their holograms representing them. The designer, Mary, is not present at the office herself either. The presentation itself is immersive. With everyone wearing AR glasses, the meeting room transforms into the new proposed office, and Mike can navigate around it. Mary drags and drops furniture and fixtures, changes colours and materials in real time. Mike and his team are presented with multiple options for the design.

As the day comes to an end and Mike and his colleagues leave the office building, the building services automatically begin to shut down in areas that are not being used. Mike's AR glasses play his favourite music and give him an update of the steps he walked today and the calories he burned, as he makes his way to the pickup point. An autonomous vehicle is about to arrive to take him back home.

The heating system at home switches on as Mike leaves the office building, so it's nice and warm as he arrives home. His smart home system connects with his AR glasses as he enters and guides him at home too, just like in the office. Mike lives alone.

As he prepares dinner, he gets an alert that the fridge is running low on milk.

'Hey Mike, you seem to be running low on milk. Current supplies are likely to last two more days. Would you like to order two weeks' supply from your Amazon account?'

Mike follows through by ordering milk and other grocery items. The smart fridge at home syncs with Mike's metaverse to maintain an updated grocery list, which is further connected to e-tailers. The fridge often suggests recipes, depending on his consumption patterns and what is in stock.

Mike, who has developed a habit of watching a late-night comedy show, is asked if he would like to watch the day's show on the giant television or as a projection through the glasses. Halfway through the show, he feels sleepy. As he retires for the night, the lights turn dim, and soothing background sounds are played for a good night's sleep. In recent years, sleep has not come easily to Mike, and he has had to depend on AI-generated ambient lighting and sounds to get his rest.

The AR glasses are wirelessly charged as Mike rests after a busy day at work.

Getting There

We are not in Mike's world yet, but it is approaching fast. From about the time Mark Zuckerberg announced, through his digital avatar, Meta's shift towards becoming a metaverse company, there has been a rush amongst other big and small players to stake their claim on building the metaverse. Many are using text generators such as ChatGPT and visual generators such as DALL-E and Midjourney, which create images out of text prompts, to build new metaverse worlds. Other tech giants occasionally throw hints about their own vision of the metaverse, and on the other, peripheral players like digital fashion brands have launched their metaverse boutiques. Gucci has created a virtual Gucci Garden. Ralph Lauren has created a virtual ski store. At the time of writing this book, many of these players have their own vision of how the metaverse will play out. It will be some time before it resembles Mike's world, but it will continue to evolve for many years as the concept of the metaverse is limitless.

Over some number of years, tech giants will fight over whose metaverse becomes dominant in which spheres. Each will sign up companies and individuals. Each is likely to have its own tie-ups with other product and service operators to build a world like Mike's. Our choices might probably be the Meta metaverse or the Microsoft metaverse or the Google metaverse. This fight-for-turf approach is likely to rule for some years before seamless integration between metaverses becomes possible—if it becomes possible.

Although the present state of worktech has a few rough edges that need to be smoothed, some of the winning concepts are clear. Relatability and ease of use are two of the main ideas that are here to stay. These will also be drivers of the metaverse. Outside the world of work, successful digital platforms have made shopping, entertainment, travel, stay and many other key aspects of our lives seem easier compared to the days of yore. The metaverse will take workers in a direction in which work will no longer feel like work, especially for knowledge workers. 'Easy work' sprouts from this.

Developments towards work-related metaverses by tech giants will require a leap of faith about how individuals will work in the future. Given the reach of these companies and their mass appeal, they often manage to influence how millions of employees work. Technology transformations by such giants are driven by, among other factors, a constant need to make things easier for their users. As big companies, they are doing the right thing for their customers and clients, and can protect and grow their market share concurrently.

While work may feel easier for some knowledge workers, it is likely that HR managers and business leaders will be faced with new challenges in managing the process of change within their organisations. Yes, the big tech companies are trying to do the right thing most of the time. However, at times, they are taking such risks that customers and clients can be left in the dust, gasping for air.

Tech transformations in the journey to the metaverse are likely to pose some new challenges for managers. For example, recent instances of employees secretly working on side hustles without informing the primary employer show their ability to be dishonest while working remotely. Dishonest behaviour is likely to increase as avatars attend meetings in the metaverse. And such dishonesty will need to be addressed.

Then, there will also be challenges related to cybersecurity and government regulations. It is quite likely that instances of data theft, money laundering, financial fraud, crimes against children, phishing and sexual assault will increase. This will also pose significant challenges for law enforcement, as most of us live in communities where law has historically been written with the physical world in mind. Not all wrongful activities conducted online come under the purview of law enforcement, as legislation does not change often enough. At the same time, not all acts that are thought of as criminal in the physical world are considered crimes when committed in the virtual world.

But because the benefits of hybrid work far outweigh the negatives, and because the tech giants have so much to gain from a healthy metaverse, changes towards a working metaverse seem inevitable.

We can't emphasise enough, though, that there will be incredible hiccups along the way to the metaverse of the future. Another of the significant fallouts of transformation is that managers will need to deal with younger generations wanting equilibrium at work. The newer generation of workers is already beginning to view the physical world differently. Because of increased time spent in virtual worlds, where digital platforms make day-to-day activities feel effortless, young workers will expect ease of use while navigating the physical world too. If working in the metaverse is replete with relatable elements and feels easy, workers will struggle if the physical office experience does not offer a similar ease of use and mental comfort.

The Metaverse's Impact on Employee Expectations

As we have established, knowledge workers are surrounded by digital platforms on a variety of devices that feed them relatable content outside work. Content can be customised to individual tastes, thanks to easy access to data about the likes and dislikes of users. Ordering tea, booking flights, watching movies, scheduling cabs and other key aspects of day-to-day living will feel effortless as experiences are curated. Curation involves pushing more and more relatable content and triggers for action. The experience of navigating such platforms feels smooth, mostly effortless and intuitive.

In recent years, workplaces have seen a significant shift with the rise of millennials and the inclusion of Gen Z in the workforce, leading to a predominant presence of digital natives. While opinions on the specific percentage of these generations in the workforce may vary, the overall trend towards a workforce dominated by tech-savvy generations is unmistakable. Gen Z is the first truly digital generation; they went online from the time they first went to school. Their sense of reality is largely determined by what digital platforms feed them. They have adapted easily to remote and hybrid work, as their general outlook towards life aligns well with the perceived ease of working on digital platforms falling under the broad umbrella of worktech. Now, different productivity and collaboration platforms are slowly being integrated and are beginning to offer personalised, relatable experiences. As the integration continues and worktech evolves to become the metaverse, offering superior experiences, a large majority of the workforce will easily adapt. Why? Because they are used to the foundation that the metaverse will be built on—their lives revolve around digital platforms offering personalised experiences.

The evolution from worktech to the metaverse is centred around algorithm-driven experiences. Based on user data, workers will get access to a superior digital workplace experience. However, the workplace journey will not be limited to putting on AR glasses and getting work done digitally. It will involve navigating the digital as well as the physical worlds. The purpose of the physical office may change, but it will not go away. People need people. Workers will still meet colleagues and clients in person. There will be days when employees will need to traverse the physical world, possibly in autonomous vehicles, to meet others in person for breakfast, for instance, then get some work done in the afternoon by collaborating with a remote team wearing AR glasses and later take a flying train back home. On the train ride, they may decide to reply to a couple of urgent emails. The workplace journey is beginning to extend far beyond the confines of the office, with a wide variety of physical and digital touchpoints. The digital touchpoints will offer superior experiences. The challenge, then, lies with the physical touchpoints.

Changing Expectations

When knowledge workers get used to relatable, customised experiences online, they will come to expect the same convenience and ease from real-world experiences. This means that there will need to be, for example, a very compelling reason for one to travel by road to the office. The full extent of the metaverse's impact is not yet visible, but we can glimpse some early signs—after long months of working completely online during the COVID pandemic, employees found it easier to work online remotely at times of their choice rather than be dictated by a nine-to-five regime of travelling to the office every day.

The rise of curated experiences in digital workplace solutions and in the metaverse soon will significantly raise employee expectations for curated experiences in the physical world. In the beginning, the metaverse experience will be superior when compared to the experience of travelling to the physical office. When a worker is in the metaverse, the online experience will be personalised, due to easy access to personalised data. For example, one may customise one's working hours dynamically based on personal choices and commitments, while the current version of the average physical office is unlikely to offer that benefit in equal measure. All of this will significantly raise the expectation of personalised experiences when one traverses the physical world.

In the future, the workplace will be the physical office, home, a coffee shop and the metaverse combined. Work will be so entwined with technology that employees will feel as if they are in a movie called 'my job'. If employee touchpoints are effectively curated in the metaverse, the same will need to be done for touchpoints in the physical world as well. Work may actually be fun on a more frequent basis, both in the physical world and the digital one.

Rise of the Right-brained Organisation

Roger Wolcott Sperry was a twentieth-century neuroscientist who won the Nobel Prize in Physiology and Medicine in 1981 for his research around the twin halves of the brain.[32] We quote from an article on the website of Simply Psychology:[33]

The brain consists of twin halves, a left hemisphere alongside a nearly symmetrical right hemisphere.

Hemispheric lateralisation is the idea that both hemispheres are functionally different and that certain mental processes and behaviours are mainly controlled by one hemisphere rather than the other.

The left hemisphere controls the right hand side of the body and receives information from the right visual field controlling speech, language and recognition of words, letters and numbers.

The right hemisphere controls the left hand side of the body and receives information from the left visual field controlling creativity, context and recognition of faces, places and objects.

Knowledge workers are paid to think and do more right-brained work. Ashu Goel, CEO at WinWire Technologies, writes about the rise of the right-brained organisation in a *Forbes* article: '...right-brained thinking also prioritizes emotion and understanding non-verbal expressions. It represents the touchy-feely part of ourselves, and its success centers on one's ability to forge meaningful and lasting business relationships.'

The rise of the right-brained organisation is also augmented by the taking over of logical, numerical, rational and repeatable tasks by left hemisphere-like algorithms. Whatever can be codified will be coded. This also means that knowledge workers will see the constant evolution of their job roles. This will involve elements of their jobs being automated.[34]

For example, before the birth of the internet, the act of sending an invoice to a client often involved typing out the invoice, printing it, then typing and printing a cover note, putting both in an envelope and then having someone make a trip to the mail room to drop it off. It probably involved a person working on it for one to two hours. Today, across industries, invoicing is automated, handled by a software application that is programmed to send out the invoice on the completion of a certain milestone. The modern way is faster than before and is almost error-free. Invoicing does not take very much work anymore.

When an element of work is taken away by algorithms, an opportunity opens up for people to spend time on right-brained problem-solving elements of work. These are often more satisfying.

Through the elimination of repetitive work, newness is introduced into job roles consistently. The coming of the metaverse means that knowledge workers will more frequently traverse from the digital to the physical worlds. Right-brained work will gain in prominence and be executed to a greater degree virtually. And almost all types of white-collar work will be a little easier.

Data for the Metaverse

For our employers to help make work become relatable, we must grant them access to data about ourselves as workers. Big data is becoming successful because, for the most part, calls for access to data are being understood. Data about past likes and dislikes of users can be utilised. Past behaviours can be understood, and the knowledge gained from this comprehension can help decide how our online existence is curated. Data should not be misconstrued as machine-generated data only. Both big data (or machine-generated data) and small data (also referred to as people data) will be important in such individual curation.

In earlier chapters, we have given examples of how Netflix has made access to entertainment feel easier and Amazon has made shopping easier. Our experiences across various online touchpoints in platforms like these feel easier because they are curated for us, thanks to the access we have given to them about our personal data and past online behaviour. In a similar fashion, metaverse touchpoints will be personalised and curated based on access to data that we make available about ourselves.

The curation of high-quality experiences across workplace touchpoints in the physical world too will need to be accomplished by drawing insights from data about workers.

Easier work will be crafted on the back of data-driven processes.

Interconnected Shifts

Our projections for success in the metaverse may come across as overly positive, perhaps even too idealistic for some readers. Despite any rosy tones, our intention is to emphasise the direction we believe to be correct: many curated experiences within the metaverse are poised to surpass their real-life counterparts. Again, we are not saying we like this. It is not a matter of our preferences; rather, it is a realistic acknowledgment of the potency of the digital world, relying upon the knowledge of what we have liked before to project what we might enjoy in the future.

This understanding sets the stage for the journey into the impact of the metaverse on employee expectations, particularly regarding curated experiences in the physical world. Unfolding like a web, this exploration reveals interconnected shifts in how we approach work and perceive our professional lives. The metaverse, we come to realise, isn't merely a technological advancement; it will act as a catalyst, reshaping the very core of what defines work. The ensuing challenge extends beyond adapting to superior digital experiences; it involves conducting a harmonious symphony between the curated metaverse and the nuanced intricacies of the physical world. This necessity for balance calls for a shift in organisational focus, which we highlight in the next chapter.

MAKING IT EASY

The Importance of Shifting the Focus

The arrival at the metaverse is perceived to be more about the journey than the destination. As technological evolution continues, given the expansiveness of innovation and the nature of the metaverse, integration of a variety of tech tools with the metaverse will give a large majority of workers a whole new experience of using their brains.

Karen Plum, Director of Research and Development at Advanced Workplace Associates, a premier workplace strategy consultancy, has researched how the brain's energies are used, especially by the average knowledge worker. She shared the diagram on the following page to explain her theories.

Whilst recognising that the brain's capacity and energy are not entirely finite, Plum says that during busy and stressful times at the workplace, many feel burnt out and exhausted, unable to tackle normal tasks, let alone more complex or innovative activities.

The human brain expends energy on a variety of tasks, as shown in the buckets. We are going to explain each of these different ways we use energy in stressful times, starting at the bottom of the bucket on the right and working our way up to the top of the bucket.

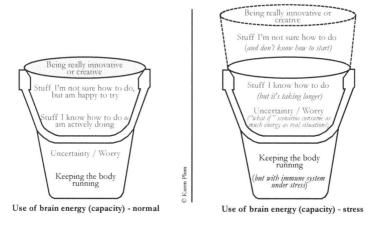

Use of brain energy (capacity) - normal   Use of brain energy (capacity) - stress

Plum's Model of Brain Energy. Copyright: Karen Plum.

Since the brain's key function is to keep our bodily systems running, it makes sense that there is a good chunk of its energy dedicated to this activity. We don't know how much, and indeed most of us are unaware of the consumption of this energy because all the work happens in the background. We don't have to consciously notice our respiratory system, for example, but nevertheless the brain must make sure it keeps working, so we stay alive.

Under periods of extreme stress or ill health, the energy required to keep us going might increase. The diagram suggests that there might be a notional maximum amount of energy available, and under different conditions, we might just run out of the additional energy needed to undertake some types of activity. Clearly, there is no actual finite amount of energy—our brains will just reprioritise to ensure the core life-sustaining activities are carried out.

If our immune system is going through a period of stress— such as during illness or when we are worried about something at work—then more energy may be needed to keep us going. Again, we don't know how much more; the diagram isn't intended to be taken literally or to indicate specific amounts of energy. So, as we press our tired brains into action, it has access to less energy.

Next come the types of activities that we know how to do. These normally require limited brain energy, particularly if they are habits or things we do regularly. Research shows that doing things in new ways, or undergoing change is metabolically expensive— novelty takes longer and requires more energy. During times of stress and anxiety, when we have less energy available, familiar tasks may also take longer and consume more energy.

Beyond the normal activities are those that are new to us. We need to draw on our resources to find ways to undertake unfamiliar tasks or tackle challenges. Perhaps given all the other demands on our energy, we simply don't have sufficient energy available for these types of tasks. Once we have consumed what seems to be the available energy, we may be concerned that we can't perform as well at work, or that we seem reluctant to take on new tasks.

Finally, there are those types of activities that call for high levels of creativity and innovation. Under normal conditions, there is some energy for these left over after other activities. Perhaps when we are absorbed by a new task, there is less time and energy required for negative emotions, such as uncertainty or worry. But under periods of intense brain energy depletion, we may be nowhere near having enough resources to be innovative or creative.

This is precisely why pressuring people to be creative will never work. Leaders ought to focus on making things easy first, before piling on work that requires employees to go down an unfamiliar path.

Plum reiterates that it is important not to take this diagram literally. Its purpose is to encourage people to recognise what is going on and to explain why they may be feeling a lack of energy and creativity, as well as an inability to cope at different times.

Shift the Focus from Motivation

Post-COVID workplace journeys for most knowledge workers include a lot of new processes, all of which take up brain space. In general, learning new tasks at work is stressful. Today's workplace journey comprises digital and physical touchpoints that are not in sync with each other, which may cause stress. Stress leads to work inefficiencies.

Many leaders understand that stress makes the workplace less productive and try to adjust by attempting to keep employees motivated. The focus is on motivation, supported by constant prompts and reminders. A lot of workers we speak with say that motivational interventions do little to alleviate stress. These workers are frustrated and see motivational interventions as being counterproductive—they don't like the preaching. In some cases, they do not appreciate the material bribes they are given and, for the most part, they would prefer that management address the root causes of stress.

It is about time leaders shifted the focus to making things easier. When the question changes from 'How do we motivate people?' to 'How do we make things easier?', the universe of options in a change rollout initiative alters.

The HR managers in a 2,000-employee office of a mid-sized corporation were struggling to get their employees back to work in offices in early 2022. They decided to offer free food as one of several lures to attract people back to headquarters. This had a marginal impact on in-office attendance. A pulse survey conducted after three months of lukewarm response showed that employees felt the food served was high in fat and sugar content, with very limited choice. Based on this and other feedback received about other material bribes, the team went back to the drawing board.

This time, it was not HR alone making the decisions. IT got involved and so did FM. A change management consultant was hired. What emerged were significantly different plans.

The collective efforts by the team of HR, IT, FM and external consultants make for an effective case study. To make the long story short, they relaunched the food programme but with healthier food. They then went a step further. They redesigned and retrofitted the office cafeteria and converted it to a food court, allowing food chains to open food stalls and sell at discounted prices. The free-food section remained, but the number of options went up, including healthy ones. Furthermore, the team had their employee app redesigned from being a seat-booking app to one that included food and transport choices. Employees could now use their app to browse through options, buy food of their choice or choose from the list of free food on offer. They could get food directly from the counter as well. They could book seats, like before, but now they could also figure out transport options for the ride home.

Interestingly, the app also allowed them to order food from a selection of chains when they worked from home. The AI-based app remembered employees' choices from the past and recommended food choices daily, based on the choices available.

Employees loved the choice and flexibility. They could get the kind of food they preferred. The situation improved for employees as they began to receive novelty, familiarity and ease of use. Ease of use, particularly, was a result of reducing the physical and mental efforts required to eat thanks to the redesigned app.

A pulse survey conducted in early 2023 showed that in-office attendance had significantly increased. This was partly attributed to the slew of new features in the employee app. Interestingly, more employees were buying food of their choice than choosing the free meal option.

This example goes to show the clear achievement of objectives when the focus shifted towards making things easier for employees rather than attempting to motivate them to behave in a certain way.

Head Towards Simplicity

Sometimes, when you find a good source of information, it is better to simply give credit where it is due. A website called Simplicable.com has a wonderful collection of ideas that help describe steps that go beyond our just cited case study.[35] Each of these themes, which we paraphrase from their website, gives new meaning to making the workplace easier for employees to navigate:

Accessibility: When giving choices to employees, the management must ensure that these options are available to everyone in the organisation. Think inclusivity. Think about different genders and the disabled. Ease of use involves designing things to the edges instead of relying on designing for the average crowd. Accessibility requires that an employer consider every touchpoint in the workplace journey and, if possible, make it easy for all categories of employees to access each benefit and advantage of the workplace.

Productivity: Employees should feel empowered by their physical surroundings and technology blending seamlessly with them. For example, every employee should be able to attend a virtual meeting in a conference room looking at a big screen but also be able to seamlessly pick up a smartphone interface and walk away from the meeting room.

Learnability: Things that are easy to learn for employees, like an employee app, can be intuitively adopted by most users.

Information: Employees need access to their files and the files of their teams, no matter where they are located. For example, the ability to access project-related information seamlessly while working from home, without the need to be in office, is incredibly important.

Ease of undo: Think of how difficult it has become to get a refund for something like a train or an airplane ticket in some cases. At times, undoing an electronic reservation at work can be just as much of a problem. Great care should be taken when using technology at work to make it easy to undo any action.

Convenience: Everyone wants systems to work for them. Many employees appreciate the ability to use the self-checkout option at the office cafeteria. This makes paying for a dessert faster than having to stand in a queue.

Maintenance: Easier systems and procedures make for good maintenance. For example, consider lighting and air conditioning systems in the office that are looped and modular. When something breaks, only the broken parts are replaced. This not only saves money but when interchangeable parts are used one can also avoid a complete shutdown.

Extensibility: Easy expansion of rooms is helpful. For instance, many employers can right-size a training room by using soundproof sliding dividers.

Compatibility: Who hasn't had problems with this type of issue? Employees love it when their gadgets work effortlessly with, for example, devices like a printer or a scanner. When a smartphone can print a document without having to download apps, it is a heavenly day.

Reliability: Clients and employees appreciate endurance and durability in workplace products. A remote server that is always up or an internet router that does not fail are two products that can make all the difference.

Think Inside the Box

Making things easier means 'thinking inside the box' sometimes, instead of pushing employees to always think outside the box. A focus on making things easier often means looking at what exists through a new pair of lenses. It underscores the importance of reevaluation and adaptation, challenging the notion that good will come largely by venturing beyond established boundaries. However, one must tread with caution and not look at making things easy in isolation. It is important to recognise that people are different—while some employees actually prefer work to not be simple, others do not want work to be simple all the time.

For example, not everyone wants work tools to be elementary. As an analogy, most smartphones offer the ease of point-and-shoot capabilities, with results that may not be easily distinguishable from those of an average DSLR camera. Although a large majority today prefer the ease of a smartphone camera, DSLR fans have not disappeared. Similarly, at work, each employee will define their own smartphone camera needs and fit into a user category. While some employees may thrive in open, collaborative areas, others find their productivity in quieter designated zones. 'Thinking inside the box' in the workplace translates to tailoring spaces and tools to diverse preferences, acknowledging that the pursuit of simplicity can coexist with individualised approaches.

The key is a balanced approach that leverages existing structures and encourages innovation. By adopting a fresh perspective on established processes, organisations can navigate the delicate balance between making work easier and respecting individual preferences, fostering a harmonious and productive work environment for all.

Changing Behaviours

With the constant need to adapt to new ways of working comes the need for individuals and groups to embrace new behaviours while letting go of some old ones. Organisational culture is built on a foundation of behaviours, with the way these behaviours are enabled and encouraged within organisations being crucial. A good organisational culture can help take an entity to new heights and, conversely, bad culture will pull almost any unit down. Behaviours cannot be left to chance in a fast-changing world of work.

The firm EY, a global leader in assurance, consulting, strategy and transactions, and tax services, talks about behaviours being the third and most important element of the three Bs—Bricks, Bytes and Behaviours. Addressing behaviours is required if one has to reimagine work. Once an organisation decides what behaviours to encourage and strengthen, it's possible to design programmes and structures around encouraging such behaviours.[36]

Our change management consulting experience has taught us to help leaders ask and answer the following questions:

- Given your vision for your entity, what will you consider as success?
- What actions must you take to ensure success?
- For such actions to be successful, what old habits must be lost?
- What new habits must be developed?
- What existing habits must be strengthened?

An effective change management initiative in organisations requires change leaders to focus not only on motivation amongst employees, but also in making the path to change easy and then supporting behaviour changes through gentle reminders and prompts. This is amplified by the Fogg Behaviour Model.

Dr B.J. Fogg founded the Behavior Design Lab at Stanford University, where he directs research and innovation.[37, 38, 39] The Fogg Behaviour Model shows that three elements must be present at the same moment for a behaviour to solidify: motivation, ability, and a prompt. Ability can be referred to as ease of use. When a behaviour does not solidify, at least one of the three elements is missing. Behaviour is the word Fogg used to describe an action that takes place. The question is how you can train employees to perform the right actions. This is the essence of behaviour design. Let us look at how it works.

In this section, we use Fogg's basic model and define key concepts.

1) *Motivation*

Fogg believes that sensation, anticipation and belonging are key terms for an understanding of motivation. Each of these three has its own distinct levels—physical, emotional and social.

Sensation: This is the physical level of motivation. The spectrum includes pleasure on one end and pain on the other. People are motivated to seek pleasure and avoid pain. The pleasure-seeker inside people enjoys games. So gamification is a very effective tactic for bringing pleasure to employees. Another means of pleasure creation is offering badges and points that encourage certain behaviours. They can work in certain industries like education platforms, online courses and training programmes, where they are used to encourage progress and acknowledge accomplishments. Conversely, industries like healthcare and legal services where the nature of work or user engagement doesn't align with gamification may find badges and points less effective.

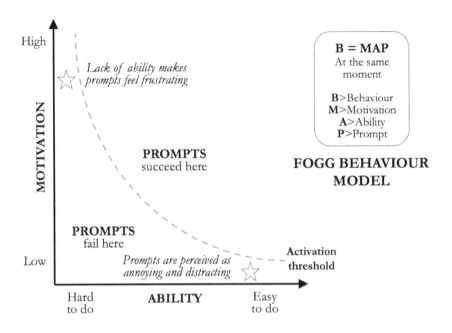

Anticipation: This is the emotional level of motivation. The spectrum runs from hope to fear. The hope of something good happening is a very powerful motivator. Tapping into the needs and aspirations of employees allows change leaders to build the desire in their employees to be part of something meaningful. When employees find meaning in what they do, they become behavioural change champions.

Belonging: This is about tapping into employees' fear of missing out (FOMO) or the social level of motivation. Employees want to feel like they belong and don't want to feel left out. Training and development programmes foster inclusion and are successful when they are social in nature. When employees feel involved in the work community, they can support each other in their quest for self-betterment.

A sense of belonging can also add to relatability. Bonding with colleagues brings familiarity and mental comfort. Encouraging bonding can lead to employees becoming less resistant to changes.

2) Ability or Ease of Use

Fogg uses the word 'ability' to mean: 'able to complete a task'. How simple a task might be is related to whether it can be completed easily. Similarly, the easier a task is to do, the higher the chances of getting it done. Fogg talks about six elements connected to how making tasks simpler encourages positive behavioural patterns. They are:

Time: No one wants to waste time. Smart managers focus on creating micro-tasks for team members. When tasks seem quick to complete, manageable and clear, they are more likely to be completed effectively.

Money: Most people are conscious of how much money they spend. The more something costs, the more they are motivated to be conscious about not spending too much. Spending what is perceived as too much money is believed to reduce the ability to accomplish an undertaking.

Physical effort: The less physical effort needs to be exerted to complete a task, the higher the chances of it getting done. People prefer automatic doors to turning door knobs. They prefer hailing cabs through an app over physically waiting by the roadside.

Thought: It's easier for people to complete tasks intuitively instead of having to exercise their brains. The less they have to think about something, the likelier it is to get done. Familiarity helps create a scenario that requires less thought.

Social deviance: People do not want to be seen as antisocial. Unlike a handful of employees, most people like to follow accepted behaviours that complete tasks effectively. They need to feel that they are part of the pack.

Non-routine: People like pattern-thinking and pattern-doing. They usually do not prefer hard tasks that fall outside of their daily routines. It is also how people structure their lives. Almost anything at work that is hard to do and falls outside of a daily routine is apt to see resistance.

3) Prompts/Triggers

Even if an employee is extremely eager to finish a straightforward task, it might still slip through the cracks. This is often because of the myriad distractions and competing priorities that characterise the professional landscape. It is not about lacking motivation; it is just life getting in the way. We all need a little nudge. Think of it like a friendly tap on the shoulder—employees need reminders to kick into gear. These prompts act as handy cues, making sure nothing slips under the radar. It is not a flaw it is a human characteristic. Prompts keep us on track and help turn intentions into accomplishments. There are three types of prompts, according to Fogg.

A spark prompt: A simple trigger that motivates employees. It works well in situations in which a task is easy to do but people are not motivated enough to do it. In a boutique consulting practice that we know, the office was designed to include several indoor plants. Employees had adopted some of these plants, as one would adopt pets. At first, the plants were being cared for well—watering them was very easy. However, the employees began to forget. And that was when one of the managers had a smart idea. They put soil moisture sensors in the pots that would prompt employees on their smartphones when their adopted plants needed watering. This worked wonders and the plants got their guardians back.

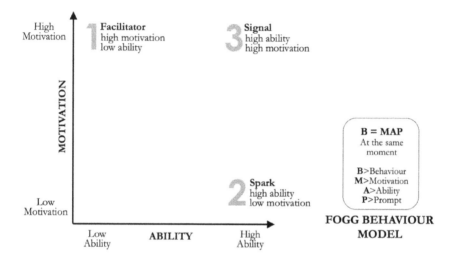

A facilitated prompt: When employees are highly motivated but they perceive a task as hard or difficult to do, a facilitated prompt acts as a helping hand. This type of prompt can go a long way in assisting them in completing the task. For instance, a highly charged-up sales team in an organisation was introduced to two different productivity tools. Adoption was low and it was discovered that the login procedure was complex. Users needed to log in twice to use the tools, and that made it rather daunting. The introduction of a facial recognition feature turned things around as the users found it effortless to log in using the new entry system. The facilitated prompt helped make it easy to use the productivity tools.

A signal prompt: Lastly, there will be situations in which employees are highly motivated to do something that is easy. They are ready; all they need is the sound of the starting gun. Once the employees hear the crack, they will start running. But no one has to pull the trigger. These types of cues are less aggressive and lead the employee to the next step in doing what needs to be done. Another way to label this is to use the nomenclature 'call to action'.

Here is a simple example. Sometimes big meetings are delayed. The last group ran over and the room must be cleaned. Often, the starter's gun does not go off for the next meeting. And people wander in over a fifteen-minute period, causing the meeting to start even later. A signal prompt can be automated in a situation such as this. A message could be automatically generated as soon as a cleaner finishes and then scans a QR code on the meeting room table, saying: 'Your meeting room is now sanitised and ready for you to occupy.'

The Fogg Behaviour Model provides a good framework to understand what triggers an employee's brain. Motivation is not easy to bring to certain situations. Many organisations spend a lot of money teaching and training people. While training is required to get people to do new things, humans are hardwired to resist certain types of hard learning. If training takes a lot of effort or time, some people will not make a complete effort to learn. Fogg suggests that to increase a user's ability, one must make the behaviour that an organisation seeks easier to exhibit. What Fogg does not suggest directly but seems to be saying, is that, along with ease of use, it is significant that users are able to find familiar elements in what they are expected to apprehend through training. This can be understood from Fogg's explanation of belonging. Remember, belonging is related to fear of missing out. When employees are called on to learn something new, they find it mentally comforting if they discover that colleagues they are familiar with are also learning the same lessons.

Persuasive Design

Fogg envisioned his behavioural concepts being helpful in the analysis and design of persuasive technologies. Such technologies are defined as those that are created to change user attitudes and behaviours through persuasion and social influence, but not necessarily through coercion.[40] Persuasive design is an area of practice that focuses on influencing human behaviour through the characteristics of a product or service. Platforms like Facebook, X (formerly Twitter), Instagram, Snapchat and TikTok are built on persuasive technology.

Tristan Harris, President and Co-Founder of the Center for Humane Technology, is quoted in the film *The Social Dilemma* as saying, '...we've moved away from having a tools-based technology environment to an addiction- and manipulation-based technology environment. That's what's changed. Social media isn't a tool that's just waiting to be used. It has its own goals, and it has its own means of pursuing them by using your psychology against you.'[41]

Technology giants focus on the confluence of motivation, ability and prompts as outlined in the Fogg Behaviour Model while designing addictive apps. The relatability factor attracts people. We want to be on social media platforms because our friends are there.

Alternatively, other companies manipulate us through other means. We may begin shopping via Amazon because we can find what we like there. But once we are logged in, Amazon's goal is to persuade us to spend more time clicking and scrolling, and consequently spending more money. The act of scrolling is a reflection of the human desire for choice, for novelty. Prompts, such as reminders that other people like us buy similar products, are other examples of how relatability also attracts us. So, as new products are introduced, the novelty factor keeps people attached to the screen. As we find that others like us buy the products, we are more likely to make the same purchases.

Similarly, apps on our smartphones, like those for shopping, travel, messaging, games and more, influence or control our actions. When we allow notifications on these apps, the app icons are marked by red dots with numbers on them. These numbers reflect the number of notifications waiting for us. The colour red is chosen because we relate red with urgency. Persuasive designers intentionally put those dots there with a number, triggering us into opening the app. As the number constantly increases, some people experience higher stress levels, and many of us end up clicking just to reduce the stress. Once you open the app, there are a host of features working behind the scenes to urge you to stay there.

For example, with messaging apps, you must have noticed the three flickering dots that indicate when the person you are chatting with is typing. The fact that you are aware they are responding makes you want to stay on. You want to see what your friend is going to say. Every minute you stay makes it more likely that you will stay the next time as well. Perhaps the reason you stay next time will be different. Big platforms have a variety of ways to keep you hooked.

One of these methods involves push notifications in social media apps. These are short messages you receive from apps when they are not open. One might say, 'Susan has tagged you in a photo.' You are thus encouraged to open the app to see the picture. You might even continue returning to the site to see if someone has commented on it. Features like these are designed to tap into our need to be socially accepted. They are intentionally put there because the designers know that we care a lot about what others think of us. These notifications are almost impossible to ignore. Look at the ease of use—all you need to do is tap and you are in.

Ease of use plays a big role in persuading people to act. In the case of streaming platforms such as Netflix and Amazon Prime Video, by auto-playing subsequent episodes of whatever we are watching, they make it easier for us to binge. In 2017, Netflix CEO Reed Hastings said at an industry summit that his company's real competitor was...sleep. 'You get a show or a movie you're really dying to watch, and you end up staying up late at night, so we actually compete with sleep,' Hastings said. 'And we're winning!'[42]

Persuasive design is based on social and psychological theories. Psychologists and behavioural science experts work together with designers to capture your attention through the characteristics of a product or an app. They work such that every tap, every ping, every notification is designed to keep you hooked. Everything is designed to feel easy.

Persuasive design does not resort to negative tactics like coercion or deception. The subtle manipulation lies in convincing users to take some action without violating their trust or irritating them with 'Please Don't Go' kinds of messages. The Fogg Behaviour Model provides a very good framework to understand how we are being manipulated. His three factors—motivation, ability and prompts—help us analyse the ways professionals are designing persuasive technologies to keep us coming back.

The Move to the Metaverse

We have established that social media is designed using persuasive technology because of its ability to influence people's attitudes and behaviours. And we have discussed how Meta, in 2021, signalled its move to become a forerunner in the metaverse landscape. We have also said that other small, medium and large tech companies are going down the same path, each wanting to capture a piece of the pie. And we have expressed our belief that the metaverse is a work in progress, and different versions of it are being created presently. The digital workplace will move to the metaverse too, and some of the products that will take us there will be Microsoft Places and Google Workplace.

The metaverse is being perceived as the possible fusion of the physical world and the virtual world. To make this vision a reality, it needs to operate a bit like our minds. Just like our brains effortlessly navigate between reality and imagination, the metaverse must seamlessly integrate both realms. It means understanding our preferences, reacting to our actions and adapting in real time. Essentially, for the metaverse to feel real, it has to work in sync with the dynamic and intricate ways our human minds effortlessly weave through the tangible and the virtual. In addition, it will probably need to show potential to alter one's sense of reality. Once this happens, human decision-making will take place within that altered reality.

Besides social media and the metaverse, AI-infused digital platforms are also focused on grabbing the attention of users. These are based on persuasive technology as well. In streaming platforms like Netflix or in e-commerce platforms like Amazon, touchpoints are curated based on the user's likes, dislikes and past choices. Personalised, relatable experiences make it easy for users to get hooked on such platforms. As users put down their AR glasses and navigate the physical world for things they cannot get done virtually, they will bring along expectations built up in the digital world. Such expectations will relate to curated experiences, ease of use, high motivation and prompts. It is worth considering the application of persuasive design principles in creating experiences in the physical world in the same ways that persuasive technologies have been used by tech giants.

The Profitability Angle

The power of AI has enabled technology platforms to become the social fabric for a large number of people. Tristan Harris, of the Center for Humane Technology, says that such platforms wield dangerous power over our ability to make sense of the world.[43] This is because thousands of engineers, designers and social and behavioural scientists work behind the scenes to alter human behaviour. There is a dark side to this, especially for impressionable young minds.

An article called 'The Risks and Dangers of Snapchat for Teens', seen on the website of Verywell Family, highlights the dangerous influence of Snapchat, a popular platform amongst teens. We quote: 'Snapchat allows users (to) send time-limited photos that might be embarrassing or just silly without a significant fear that an image will find its way to other social media sites where it might live forever. With Snapchat, teens have a way to interact that feels authentic and fun.'[44]

Built into Snapchat is a feature called Snapstreak. 'A Snapstreak is when two users have snapped back and forth within a 24-hour period for three days in a row. Once this occurs, a flame emoji and a number will appear next to the names of the users to show how long the streak has been maintained. Maintaining streaks is very important to teens because streaks allow kids to interact socially and feel part of something many of their peers are doing. For many kids, they're a measure of their friendships.' A fire emoji next to someone's name is often seen as an extremely meaningful indicator of friendship. Sociologists worry that children's sense of friendship is being altered, such that it turns dependent on the metrics of this app.

The situation becomes worrisome when one's sense of reality

is influenced by a flame emoji. Individuals take actions based on all kinds of inputs. Sometimes they act without realising that their sense of reality is altered. This happens because persuasive design taps into the deepest reaches of the brain.[45]

Stanford University started the Persuasive Tech Lab in 1997, a testimony to the power of persuasion. Technology platforms will continue to spend billions of dollars swaying the behaviour of millions of users because of the potential profits they can make. The longer they can hold your attention, the more money they can earn. Experts see an unethical slant with many of these platforms. Harris feels that it can be ethical to make these types of profits when the goals of the persuaded and the goals of the persuader are the same. Often, however, they are not. Many are recognising this and are starting to stand up to the big firms. People like Tristan Harris are educating others about manipulative design features and their psychological impact. Regulators are pushing for transparency in algorithms and design decisions from tech giants. Others are opting out of platforms that exploit attention for profit.

It's Not Just About Selling Stuff

Persuasive design need not be only about selling stuff and making profits.

Within organisations, when something new is introduced, HR departments focus on building motivation and encouraging employees through new policies, training sessions and reminders. Often, change makes employees feel threatened, and sometimes they push back. Change triggers a primal fear of the unknown, rooted in our survival instinct. People resist by clinging to familiarity, exhibiting denial, scepticism or outright rejection. This resistance is a natural human response, serving as a protective shield against perceived threats to stability and competence in the face of the unfamiliar. When something new is introduced, what workers don't like is being lectured and feeling manipulated. But just as how tech giants design user behaviour, employees do not seem to mind when persuasive technologies are used to make their jobs easier.

Another theme in organisational life that bothers employees relates to when they receive too many internal surveys. As we all know, organisations conduct many surveys to get a sense of how employees are feeling. Getting a large majority of employees to fill out these surveys usually takes more than one reminder.

Many managers complain that the response rate to these surveys is so low as to make the surveys invalid for almost all purposes. Some managers have said that they don't understand why employees avoid filling them out when the surveys are really for their good.

One particularly smart manager told one of us that when she was trying to measure the success of a hybrid work policy recently, instead of conducting another survey asking employees to fill in details such as number of hours at a desk or at home, etc., she decided to pull in the central data points from existing systems her company already had in place. The employee app that allowed them to book seats and other facilities had already collected the needed information about user preferences and where they sat. Sensors collected the other data that was needed. Between the app and the sensors, she could access information that allowed her to skip many of the questions she would have asked the employees in the past.

Managers often seem to be making employees do unnecessary tasks. Understandably, this frustrates employees, as they see managers using legacy methods even after new ways are available.

In the case just discussed, the manager simply used information from different sources to collect data on hybrid work. She didn't need to ask employees to fill out another long survey.

It probably goes without saying, but employees don't like to be asked to do unnecessary tasks. Persuasive design works for big tech companies because it creates a situation where users are not asked to do anything. Users take action and share information without realising, in some cases, what led them to do so. There is a lot of subtlety involved with persuasive design.

Persuasion and Manipulation: Two Different Things

Sometimes, the most pressing problems in life can be set aside for a while as a social media platform engages a troubled soul with content that makes them feel good—for example, watching puppies play on Facebook. But what has become apparent over the last several years is that having our opinions validated by our social media feeds is also a way to feel good in the short term. Tristan Harris says that our brains are not wired for truth-seeking—information that confirms our beliefs makes us feel good; information that challenges our beliefs doesn't. This is why people are shown more of what they agree with on their smart devices. The internet is flooded continually, but especially at election time, by polarising information that works to accomplish its goals to keep individuals believing what they believe. Citizens often only see feeds that support their side of a polarised debate.

A scary fact is that the metaverse is being built on top of these learnings. Irrespective of whether one uses the metaverse for recreation or for work, one can feel confident that it will be curated to tap into personal likes. This will make sure it endures. When the metaverse is used by some employers across the globe to be the go-to place to work, other companies will notice. They will join others that start conducting work on the metaverse. One of the main reasons for doing so is that they will find that more and more of their current employees, and many of the prospective employees they want to hire, will find it difficult to navigate a physical work environment in which experiences are not as personalised as they will be on the metaverse. And they will find that many of those same employees and prospective employees won't appreciate having their beliefs challenged. Our belief is that many companies will become more homogenised around the ways employees think. This shift reinforces a collective mindset within companies, aligning employees around shared beliefs and preferences. The metaverse-driven homogenisation is likely to emerge organically, driven by a desire for comfort and affirmation, both in work-related functions and societal perspectives.

So persuasive design is very powerful. We don't look forward to living in a world where it is used even more than it is today, but if the profit motive and politics are taken out of persuasive design, a lot of good can come out of it. The same techniques of persuasive design can be used to, first, give employees personalised experiences in meaningful, purpose-driven companies, and, second, to solve problems that need to be solved around the world, by all types of organisations.

Persuasive design is not a familiar concept with many corporates. Often, in casual conversation with business leaders, when we bring up the term, a common reaction is, 'Oh design, that is not for me.' Many of those who are aware of the discipline perceive it as a technique that is used to sell products online. The knee-jerk reaction to this understanding is to pull away.

Jeff Horvath, in his paper 'Persuasive Design: It's Not Just About Selling Stuff', digs around to find out why leaders react negatively to the topic[46] and helps us understand why. His takeaways are that leaders do not like to be seen as selling something in a manipulative way. And he cites managers who feel that persuading is akin to tricking. Leaders, understandably, often like to take the high moral ground by not tricking their employees or customers.

It is really important to distinguish between persuasion and manipulation. Manipulation implies deception and coercion. All efforts to deceive should end in rejection and distrust. Perpetrators should not be able to easily recover. But to use relatability, familiarity and a sense of the preferences and likes of employees can be beneficial to all.

Persuasive Design in the Non-Virtual World

In their 2008 book *Nudge: Improving Decisions About Health, Wealth, and Happiness*, Richard H. Thaler and Cass R. Sunstein talked about nudging people towards making better decisions.[47] They give the example of the director of food services at a large city school system being concerned about the nutritional value of the food the children were eating and the choices they were making. She could decide exactly what food would be available to the children, but she knew that providing the kids with choices was important to getting them to eat and be happy about eating at school.

The director tried an experiment. She varied the placement of different food and the order in which they were displayed. She put food she wanted the children to eat at eye level in the dispensaries where they picked up their food. She varied what the kids saw first and what they saw last. In the end, she discovered that she could increase or decrease the consumption of certain types of food by as much as 25 per cent! By designing the food selection process in different ways, she met her goal of nudging the kids to eat healthier without restricting their choices or reducing their satisfaction. Through some wise design choices, she could increase the wise eating conversion rate.

Persuasion techniques have been used in the retail and hospitality industries for a long time. As offices become more and more like lounges and malls, there is much to learn from these two industries.

Devangi Vivrekar, in her thesis *Persuasive Design Techniques in the Attention Economy: User Awareness, Theory, and Ethics,* submitted at Stanford University, touches upon the uses of persuasion techniques in the retail and hospitality industries.[48] For example, she urges us to notice how architectural elements in casinos include maze-like paths that create the illusion of small, secluded spaces. She also points out the apparent lack of exits. All of these attributes, in subtle ways, persuade people to stay and continue spending money.

To return to food as an example, visual cues about food portion size influence how much people eat. With obesity becoming an issue in many parts of the world, various types of initiatives are often undertaken to facilitate healthier (often meaning smaller portion) eating. However, telling people to eat smaller portions does not always achieve the desired results. Who wants to be told?[49] Frequent visual exposure to smaller portion sizes in pictures reconstructs the mind's perceptions of what a normal-sized portion of food should be. As people are consistently shown visuals of smaller portions, their needs change, and over time they begin to partake less without anyone asking them to do so.

Similarly, placebo buttons are often placed at or on crosswalks, elevators and thermostats. These deliver a sense of control without actual functionality. The crosswalk buttons may discourage jaywalking. The close buttons on an elevator may make you feel that the doors are closing faster. And many thermostats, especially in hotels, simply give a sense of changing temperature to someone pushing a button, when, in fact, there is no connection between pushing that button and anything changing. Toilet flush controls with dual buttons encourage users to conserve water. We like it more when we feel like we are actually making a difference in all of the right ways, rather than just being fooled into thinking that something has happened.

Persuasive Design in the Workplace Journey

We think we have built a fairly strong argument that the path along which worktech is progressing towards the metaverse is being built on persuasive design techniques. This is a natural progression from the learnings of successful user-centric digital platforms. In hybrid work, knowledge workers will encounter workplace touchpoints in the digital world as well as in the physical world. Workers will experience superior personalised digital tools. And these tools will be so easy to use that even the least intuitive people will be quick to adapt to them. When employees navigate the physical world, they will have completely reasonable expectations of personalised, relatable experiences at work. But to make all of this possible, leaders need to look at the workplace journey as a combination of digital and physical touchpoints. They will need to work on making physical touchpoints easy to navigate by deploying persuasive design techniques. Organisations that are able to dynamically make work easier will have a strategic advantage and will be able to attract and retain scarce talent better than others.

Over time, tech companies will work with client organisations to co-create customised digital touchpoints that understand workers and help them navigate a workday effortlessly. If an employee's smartwatch picks up the signs of an elevated body temperature one morning, technology should be able to automatically trigger a series of actions, like informing the employee's boss, cancelling meetings, prompting and helping identify the right physicians to consult. All the technology needed to pull this off is already available. The future will see these being integrated.

A DATA-DRIVEN APPROACH

The Employee as a Customer

Making things easy is also a primary driver in user design, and involves two broad factors.[50, 51, 52] You will recognise these as they are very similar to the factors that drive persuasion theory: **relatability,** or making it easy for the mind to adopt something new by introducing familiar elements, and **ease of use or ability**, meaning how simple it is for someone to do something at a particular moment in time.

Experience designers strive to answer questions like these four:

1. How can users easily relate to it?
2. How can we introduce something that users are familiar with?
3. Can users interact easily enough with the touchpoint to complete their tasks effortlessly?
4. How might we minimise the complexity of what users must do to complete a task?

Ease of use is an integral part of a seamless user experience. This chapter is about how employees are users too. For us, it is particularly important to examine how users experience the workplace. Organisations spend billions of dollars in understanding the needs and aspirations of customers. Why not take a similar approach while spending much less money on the needs and aspirations of employees?

Consumer marketing has conventionally taken progressive approaches to understanding the needs of customers and users, with support from digital design addressing the needs of people who want to make purchases. This involves designing experiences around the use of a product or service and is at the base of marketing strategy, requiring in-depth research. There's no reason that thinking of employees as customers and crafting employee experiences in the same vein should be considered as anything but helpful. Achieving business goals by fulfilling employee expectations in this manner should be seen as a huge victory.

'If we have a Customer Experience Group, why not create an Employee Experience Group?' asks Mark Levy, the global head of employee experience at Airbnb. The online travel company converted its traditional HR groups into an employee experience team. Airbnb's business is built around the concept of making people feel at home anywhere. And Airbnb wanted to offer employees the same level of experience that it offers to its customers.[53]

Although the employees-as-customers narrative has existed for more than four decades, its adoption has not been very wide. The COVID pandemic brought to the fore a very bitter pill to swallow for employers—employees have much more power than managers imagined. They have many more career options today than ever before. They can go to a competitor as a regular worker, as a part-time worker or as a remote worker. This is one reason why the customer/employee comparison is more valid today. Customers have always had choices. Employees are just realising theirs.

In contrast to many organisations whose employees are

A Data-Driven Approach   129

leaving, some employees develop a sense of ownership about their employer when they feel valued and appreciated, beyond the transactional nature of the employer–employee relationship. Clearly communicating that the employer organisation's existence is intricately tied to its employees cultivates a foundation of mutual trust and respect. These employees often go beyond the call of duty at work. They feel they are not just a cog in the wheel and are convinced of their employer's goodness as they are treated differently than others who worked elsewhere. Looking at employees through the lens of a customer enables organisations to bond with employees.

A Holistic Approach

As with customers, today's employees are aware of and have access to options. This forces traditional organisations to rethink how they can stay ahead of the game.

The old ways of talent management, which involved on-boarding fresh talent and off-boarding retirees was steeped in industrial-era thinking. Standardisation and scale dominated. However, that approach does not work anymore. Just as how consumer product companies have evolved from using mass marketing tactics to now using customised push advertising, contemporary organisations need to move beyond a one-size-fits-all approach when it comes to employees.

Also, the COVID era in HR is over. In the post-COVID era, organisations must ditch one-size quick fixes for employee issues. A holistic approach is now essential. Laszlo Bock, former head of Google's People Operations, says, 'We all have our opinions and case studies, but there is precious little scientific certainty around how to build great work environments, cultivate high-performing teams, maximize productivity, or enhance happiness.'[54] We believe Bock's statement is true—HR, FM and IT teams need to work together to carve out holistic solutions for personalised workplace experiences to be delivered. But we don't have solid evidence that we are right. We just have over hundred years' worth of experience that tells us we are heading in the correct direction.

Take a moment to reflect upon the following. While choosing persuasive design techniques, focusing on making things easy and relatable for employees will buttress already evolved HR processes of building motivation and prompting users. This will in turn pave the path for employees to take action to change behaviours, which will help them achieve their goals. Further, a shift to looking at employees as customers will necessitate organisations to think anew about the design of workplace experience journeys. Using persuasive design techniques will sync well with the latent employee expectation of personalised experiences.

Using a Data-driven, Agile Approach

How do we move forward to make workplaces relatable and simple? How do we make things easier at work? These questions can best be answered when a user-centric approach is being implemented. Such an approach involves the following five steps:

1. **Research**: Research the needs and aspirations of employees. This involves collating dynamic data about employees to understand changing aspirations.
2. **Recognise**: Recognise patterns in the data collected to define problems and positive trends correctly.
3. **Ideate**: Challenge assumptions. Identify gaps, if any, between employee aspirations and leadership vision. Prioritise ideas that make things easy.

4. **Pilot**: Continuously prototype and test limited versions of planned transformation initiatives.

5. **Implement**: After learning from the prototyping and testing, roll out initiatives.

Sudden changes, like those caused by the COVID pandemic, often mean having to skip the first three steps mentioned here. Emergencies require emergency measures. However, at other times, it is decisive that all attempts are made to understand the true aspirations and needs of employees. This begins with collecting non-private data about employees, which involves combing through a combination of small data (or people data) generated via surveys, interviews and focus groups, as well as whatever big data is available from sensors, beacons, apps, etc. A successful data-driven approach also involves spot-checking data as steps 4 and 5 are undertaken to collate dynamic data. This is done in order to understand changing aspirations, needs and behaviours. Spot-checking allows leaders to take informed decisions dynamically.

Any organisational change initiative that results in alterations in workplace journeys or touchpoints can be called a workplace transformation initiative. It won't come as any surprise, given that we have discussed this, that we believe the introduction of a new remote work policy or a redesign of an office or a move to a new office location are all transformational. Workplace transformation initiatives often involve tweaking factors that impact worker performance as well as factors related to real estate efficiency. An organisation's bottom line has a heavy dependency on both. Using a data-driven approach makes it easier to be objective about decisions.

Informed workplace strategies, supported by robust data analysis, instil confidence in decision-making processes. By leveraging comprehensive data, it becomes possible to make precise predictions regarding evolving work styles and the future landscape of real estate portfolios. Analysing trends and patterns allows for a nuanced understanding of how work environments will adapt, enabling organisations to proactively align their real estate assets with upcoming needs. This foresight not only optimises resource allocation but also ensures that real estate investments are strategically aligned with the dynamic nature of the workforce, fostering agility and resilience in the face of ever-changing business environments. Such approaches also help spot trends and opportunities sooner, resulting in organisations that are more agile and efficient. Real-time measurement of data allows quick course corrections if necessary. Besides these benefits, and the fact that such an approach paves the way towards easier work, what we recommend has many more rewards:

Greater confidence in employee- and workplace-related decisions: Data-driven insights replace subjective opinions about erstwhile fuzzy areas like employee desires and behaviours. Data analysis provides clarity that intuition and opinion do not. A data-backed workplace strategy can demonstrate the impact of decisions. It can also mitigate doubts around leadership vision and how that aligns with employee aspirations.

Agility and scalability: Setting up a body within an organisation to secure dynamic data around employee behavioural trends, office occupancy rates, infrastructure performance, etc., helps establish goals and measure results. Trend analysis helps make tweaks if necessary and improves employee and infrastructure performance. New ideas can be implemented faster with good data. And this all feeds the possibility of continuous, incremental changes and improvements that make an organisation more agile and help it to scale faster.

Cost savings and operational efficiency: A data-driven approach brings accountability. Specific goals can be set and results can be measured. These bring higher efficiency and cost savings. In a hybrid work model, analysing occupancy trends becomes instrumental in identifying the specific types and sizes of office real estate needed. HR managers and facility managers can use this information to make informed decisions based on real-time evidence. Data analysis can help reduce waste and inefficiencies and derive increased value from existing assets.

Employee ownership and engagement: A data-based approach makes the rationale behind decisions clear. This makes it easier to convince employees to take the right actions, reducing the scope for adamant positions based on ego and opinion. Moreover, collecting and analysing people data obtained through surveys, focus groups and interviews infuses a sense of ownership amongst employees about decisions. They feel heard. This boosts loyalty and can raise morale. A data-driven approach helps employees see clear goalposts, giving them a sense of control over things.

Data-oriented planning helps improve teamwork, employee engagement and organisational consistency. Each of these makes it easier to retain scarce talent.

A Data-backed Workplace Strategy

To recap, an employee experience journey is the progression of an employee across different organisational touchpoints. In the hybrid work model, touchpoints can be encountered within and outside an office, and vary from having lunch in the office cafeteria and an online interaction over a digital platform to booking meeting rooms via an employee app and more. Delivering a superior workplace journey begins with the understanding that the employee experience journey differs from person to person.

We now live in a world where every knowledge worker will, in their lifetime, get the choice to work remotely, and each one of these workers will need a slightly different combination of assists from their organisations.

With choice in their hands, the workplace journey for employees begins with an option of working from the office or from a remote location. Working from home takes them on a workplace journey that is clearly different from that of working from the office. While policies and communication, backed by prompts, help build high motivation levels, making things easy at every touchpoint on a chosen workplace journey requires real planning in most organisations.

Be it driving on the freeway or surfing social media feeds, people like to do things intuitively. In fact, the technology used also needs to be intuitive as employees work virtually. Organisations have to make the touchpoints work for employees in an increasingly personalised way in the digital age, especially as workers use their homes as their workplaces. To move close to the level of personalisation required, organisations need a roadmap for the future. We are convinced that the roadmap has to begin with a workplace strategy.

A workplace strategy provides a blueprint to get the most out of an organisation's people, its technology and its places, tightly tuned to the business objectives, desired behaviours and culture. When a strategy is backed by data, it is easier to implement, especially for the four questions we introduced at the beginning of this chapter. Once implemented, a good workplace strategy can respond dynamically to the changing aspirations and behaviours of employees. This, in our opinion, is what leads to easy work, and helps develop agility and resilience in organisations and the teams within.

Defining the Path to Easy Work

Mark Dixon, founder and CEO of International Workplace Group (IWG), a UK-based office space firm, says this about the physical office where people collect: 'It's a place with their name over the door. It gives people a sense of belonging. To get rid of it is like having an army that doesn't have a basecamp. You must have a place to bring your army together.'[55]

Offices are being re-imagined globally. For different organisations, they serve different purposes. Besides allowing for spaces within the office that facilitate work requiring deep focus, following are three of the most commonly heard purposes of the physical office these days.

A space where ideas collide: The office is being increasingly seen as a place where employees are inspired and motivated by sharing ideas with colleagues in-person.

A home for boosting company culture: Physical spaces allow leaders and others to systematically reinforce company culture. In-person team-building exercises, talks, learning opportunities, seeing others at work, etc., help boost motivation and build culture.

A place for employees to socialise: People need people. That is a basic human trait. The physical office provides a great opportunity for employees to bond with one another.

The physical office is, it almost goes without saying, an integral part of the entire workplace journey. The purpose of the office is well-entrenched as a place to do things that cannot be effectively done virtually. Human activities, such as collaboration and socialising, are most effective when conducted in person. From an employer's standpoint, these aspects hold the potential for a strategic advantage in attracting and retaining talent. In the hybrid

work scenario, discerning between workplace experiences provided
by rival organisations becomes challenging, particularly for those
entering the workforce during the era of hybrid work. This
difficulty arises because they may have predominantly interacted
with colleagues over laptops, making it a more influential factor
in shaping the company culture than in-person interactions. The
modern workplace stands at the intersection of the physical and the
digital, where both realms play pivotal roles in fostering a thriving
and interconnected professional environment.

Welcoming this integration enables organisations to establish
a comprehensive and flexible work environment that addresses
evolving and diverse needs. As the management of this hybrid
workplace continually becomes more refined, frequent workplace
transformations unfold. With such transformations becoming
increasingly common, the strategic use of big data and small data
analytics becomes progressively crucial. This empowers leaders to
make well-informed decisions, elevating both operational efficiency
and employee experiences.

Data in a Workplace Transformation Initiative

Any organisational initiative that results in changes in workplace
journeys or touchpoints can be called workplace transformation.
Examples could be the introduction of new ways of working
defined by a remote work policy, the redesign of an office or a
move to a new office location. Making the workplace journey
smooth and easy requires an understanding of how a data-oriented
approach can be actioned at different stages of a workplace
transformation project. A workplace transformation initiative that
centres around making work easier draws on non-private employee
data throughout the five steps mentioned in the chapter titled 'The

Employee as a Customer'. The pages from here on explain, in a step-by-step manner, how a data-driven approach can be applied at each stage to deliver superior workplace experiences. Readers and practitioners may use this as a broad framework and customise the combination of activities to make them relevant to their workplace transformation initiative.

Use of Small Data in the Beginning

Early research is required to elicit both the aspirations of the employees and the leadership's vision. Analysis of such information allows one to understand these two components and draw up a strategy that brings together business goals with the needs and aspirations of employees as best as possible. Workplace strategists take the lead at this stage and collect data required through a variety of activities like surveys, infrastructure reviews, interviews and focus groups. Such data is referred to as people data or small data. Occasionally, some organisations may have access to past occupancy data, which can aid in determining work patterns for a new office.

The data collected usually leads to insights that can be used to determine a workplace strategy. A workplace strategy is like a blueprint for the newly imagined workplace and becomes a guiding star for interior designers, HR leads and organisational leaders to streamline their respective processes and plans.

Leadership finds it helpful to align office design and IT strategy to complement HR policies, ensuring that people are happy and satisfied at work. A desire to understand the aspirations of employees enables human centricity in design. The office design thus becomes evidence-based and has a far higher chance of success than one that is not based on evidence and data.

A good office design is one that is empathetic to the needs of employees and aligned to meeting business goals. Offices set up in the post-COVID world are seeing the inclusion of automatic data collection tools like occupancy sensors and thermal cameras that help with the real-time curation of employee experiences in the office. The data collected is used to improve office facilities and the employee experience journey.

Use of Big Data Once the Workplace Transformation Is Implemented

The physical office serves different purposes, one of which is work. Progressive organisations believe in curating employee experiences in the office that are not centred just around work. Such organisations believe that the office can enable and fulfil other needs of the employees, such as socialisation and wellness. During a typical day, the average employee constantly moves between one part of the progressive office to another, depending on the task at hand. Such movement also varies from department to department and person to person. Just as how social media feeds adapt the content you receive based on your likes and geography, the office too can respond, in real time, to suit team and individual preferences. This becomes possible with the use of a variety of sensors that monitor, for instance, occupancy, temperature, air quality, light, the nuances of people's movement, the movement of the sun and other aspects of the environment. Such real-time data is sent to the cloud, where pre-programmed algorithms allow the infrastructure to respond based on dynamic information.

A simple example of this is an air conditioning system turning on as an employee begins to use a work pod. A complex version of temperature setting will, in the future, adjust automatically to the degree-setting preferred by the employee, based on their previous selections, how they are dressed and any other variable that is deemed important. This is just one application of the abilities of the IoT, algorithms and big data becoming operational in the physical office.

The use of big data in the office will be broad and deep. AI tools can not only predict the next date an employee is likely to be in the office but can also recommend future dates when that same person ought to be physically present at work. Such recommendations are the result of analysing past records of the employee's visits in relation to the patterns of team members with whom they collaborate. The richness of such data can be further enhanced by integrating transportation and parking options, food choices, etc.

Mixed Use of Small and Big Data for Course Corrections

Things almost never go as planned. Across different organisational patterns, during the life cycle of an office, the business environment changes rapidly, and so do people's aspirations. Given the dynamic nature of all this, the ways workplaces need to support their users keep changing. So course corrections occur and realignments become inevitable. Given that the twofold primary purpose of any business is clear—to make money and to serve stakeholders— business-related course corrections are primarily based on stakeholder analyses, which are often numbers-oriented. Similarly, changes required in the office infrastructure ought to be based on numbers, that is, supported by data.

The installation of data-capturing devices within offices, along with data about an employee's choices captured from employee apps, allows organisations to be much more flexible. For example, with data on workspace utilisation and parking availability readily accessible, organisations can optimise their resources efficiently. This flexibility enables a more responsive and adaptable approach to accommodate changing work patterns, fostering a seamless and user-friendly experience for employees while maximising the efficiency of office spaces and amenities. Trend analysis of such data can be very helpful as well.

Analysing trends in such data proves valuable too. For example, the data might indicate that an organisation chooses to terminate a lease midway through a three- or five-year agreement. Even when a lease runs its full term, and an organisation decides to sign up for a new office space, a combination of big and small data analysis can enable reliable and accurate decisions. This type of analytic ability reduces the need for frequent course corrections.

This brings the first part of the book to an end. We have built on the importance and effectiveness of making work easier. The second part presents action items for the workplace, and we expect that if you follow these steps, you will have an easier place to work. We are not saying it will be easy to change your work culture or processes. But we are saying that our suggestions will make it simpler.

Part 2 | THE HOW

PREPARING THE ORGANISATION

Refer to the Vision and the Mission

No good workplace transformation initiative can go forward unless it is consistent with the organisation's mission. While preparing for a workplace transformation initiative, it is critical that the team behind it refers to the mission statement and understands it completely. If there is no dedicated workplace management team, human resources (HR), corporate real estate (CRE) or relevant leaders can collaborate to handle this responsibility.

Senior leadership in organisations often gives direction via mission statements that are refreshed every few years. Mission statements are usually based on vision statements, which provide a brief description of an organisation's long-term goals. On the other hand, a mission statement focuses on the present—it defines the customers and critical processes, and it states the desired level of performance. This makes it a critical document when proceeding with workplace transformation plans.

A few focus group workshops involving senior leadership and workplace management leaders may be required to develop a comprehensive understanding of the mission statement. Such discussions are effective when outcomes include establishing shared concepts around the mission, influences of the mission statement on the workplace transformation initiative and agreement on high-level goals for it.

The workshops also provide an opportunity to revisit the organisation's core values. Core values encapsulate the fundamental beliefs that shape organisational culture. Integrating these values into the transformation framework fosters a workplace environment that aligns with the principles deemed essential by the organisation. Thus, the initiative not only reflects the current mission but also embodies the enduring values that define the organisation's identity. Regular reflection on both mission and values ensures a holistic and enduring approach to workplace transformation, and also sees to it that the transformation stays in sync with the organisation's overarching goals.

Change is never easy, and an organisation needs to prepare itself before embarking on transformation. Once the above are established, the right team ought to be chosen for the initiative. This may involve expanding the existing workplace management team or creating a new specialised team.

Set Up Goals and a Team

Refurbishing the office and integrating digital collaboration and efficiency tools are huge expenses. However, this spending pays back, not only in terms of measurable savings in energy, time and real estate but also by supporting business needs and employee needs—a far greater return. However, the tables turn if the physical and the digital infrastructure are unable to support broader business needs in an integrated manner. The huge payback on serving business requirements will be lost if the infrastructure plan is shortsighted. Worse still, if the infrastructure is misaligned with serving such exigencies, it may even harm people's morale and work efficiency. Remember, people resist change, however good it may be for them. When swanky new infrastructure is thrust upon employees, they may—rightfully—get upset if it is not aligned with their aspirations.

Workplace transformation needs to be undertaken holistically. For this to happen, the transformation needs to be driven by a specialised team comprising multi-disciplinary team members. Implementation is no more about simply building new infrastructure or deploying a new piece of fancy technology—it must include a layer of change management and needs to be managed delicately, driven by the team set up for the purpose.

To act holistically, a workplace management team might begin, once it has received its big-picture marching orders, by asking the question: 'What problem are we trying to solve?' The risk of not doing this is a possible rush to a solution without clearly defining the problems. When teams representing various skill groups and departments meet and the problem is defined before the solution is hatched, holistic answers will almost always emerge.

Facility Management to Workplace Management

Companies born in an era when the workplace meant the physical office usually has a facilities management (FM) department. Sometimes FM works closely with the corporate real estate (CRE) department. Often the HR department is also deeply involved with workplace design, while the IT department will be involved in any meaningful tech transformation. Although there will be many instances of these, let us look at three where we often see the need for integration leading to collaboration:

Digital security and physical security integration:

- **Collaboration:** IT and FM collaborate to ensure a cohesive approach to security, both in the digital and physical realms.
- **Integration:** HR supports by implementing policies and training programmes that align with security measures, fostering a culture of security awareness among employees.

Employee well-being initiatives:

- **Collaboration**: HR and FM collaborate on initiatives that enhance employee well-being, such as ergonomic workspace design and health-focused amenities.
- **Integration**: IT supports these initiatives by providing tools like a wellness feature in employee apps or incorporating technology solutions that promote work–life balance.

Space utilisation and employee experience:

- **Collaboration**: FM and HR collaborate on assessing and optimising space utilisation based on employee needs and preferences.
- **Integration**: IT contributes by leveraging data analytics

to gather insights on technology usage, contributing to a holistic understanding of the overall employee experience.

Working together leads to the emergence of workplace management as a crucial cross-party function. To recap, Workplace Evolutionaries describes workplace management as '...a dynamic, emerging discipline that designs and delivers an organisation's unique workplace experience, aligning it to strategic drivers and business goals'.

Workplace management as a discipline is successful not only when it leads specialised projects but when it also monitors the performance of a workplace on an ongoing basis. This requires that the criteria for success be determined, which can be done through a series of structured focus-group workshops bringing together individuals who are representative of every layer of the organisation. As before, once data is collected, it needs to be analysed thoroughly. Pulse surveys need to be conducted as well to gauge the performance of the workplace. Depending on the results of these, course corrections may be introduced if necessary.

A Workplace Management SPOC

The functional dependencies between FM, HR and IT departments have become more than obvious in a post-pandemic world. Besides the three instances cited a few paragraphs earlier, such interdependencies are many and multi-layered and are often linked to issues that may require senior-leadership intervention.

A team that works on such issues usually runs projects with the identification of a single point of contact (SPOC). The SPOC is responsible for defining individual roles and giving direction to the initiative. But increasingly, many organisations are beginning to view workplace management as a discipline that requires multi-disciplinary teams to engage in the day-to-day running of the workplace, given that frequent changes are the order of the day. In the new age, no one person can run the services of workplace management in a large organisation that is addressing cross-disciplinary issues.

Take Outside Help when Forming Teams

Not every organisation may have the bandwidth to set up a workplace management team suddenly, even if that is the need of the hour. Seek outside help if required. Workplace management as a discipline is becoming more and more mainstream by the day and there are consultants who offer their services to help make transitions.

Reasons to delegate to external help may include:

- **Immediate need**: When the organisation faces urgent workplace challenges requiring prompt action and forming an in-house team is time-prohibitive.
- **Lack of internal expertise**: In instances where the organisation lacks internal proficiency in workplace management, particularly when dealing with multi-disciplinary issues and transitions.
- **Resource constraints**: Limited financial or human resources may hinder the establishment and maintenance of an internal workplace management team.
- **Specialised knowledge**: External consultants often possess specialised knowledge and experience in workplace management, offering valuable insights and best practices.

When selecting a service provider for workplace management, organisations should seek:

- **Expertise in workplace management**: A service provider with a proven track record and proficiency in designing and implementing effective workplace management strategies.
- **Cross-disciplinary capabilities**: The capability to comprehend and address multi-disciplinary issues involving FM, HR, IT and other pertinent departments.
- **Adaptability and agility**: The ability to adjust to the dynamic nature of workplace changes and provide agile solutions in response to evolving organisational needs.
- **Collaborative approach**: A collaborative approach in working with internal teams, fostering effective communication and coordination.
- **Customisation**: The ability to tailor solutions to the specific needs and culture of the organisation, avoiding one-size-fits-all approaches.
- **Change management expertise**: Proficiency in change management processes, recognising that workplace management often entails significant organisational transitions.

By carefully considering these factors, organisations can make informed decisions when seeking external help for workplace management. This ensures a seamless transition and the establishment of practices aligned with the organisation's goals and objectives.

Take the Design-thinking Approach

Following the design-thinking approach to identify and solve a problem is a tried-and-tested way to work.

Design thinking is a problem-solving iterative process that prioritises empathy, creativity and collaboration to address complex challenges. It involves understanding user needs, ideating potential solutions, prototyping and iterating based on feedback. Focused on human-centred solutions, design thinking encourages a mindset that values experimentation and learning from failures. Commonly used in product and service development, this approach fosters innovation by placing end users at the forefront, ensuring solutions are not only functional but also resonate with the human experience.

In the context of this book, empathy is at the core, other things pivoting off it. Empathy involves developing a deep understanding of the needs of employees. Unintended negative consequences are a frequent outcome of human resource and facilities decisions. Design thinking can help identify problems before they occur.

Design thinking is also very useful when it comes to tackling problems that are ill-defined. By re-framing these problems in human-centric ways, it becomes possible to develop ideas in brainstorming sessions. Thereafter, the sessions allow a hands-on approach to prototyping, testing and ongoing experimentation.

If all the frills of service businesses are removed, most of these organisations are likely to be successful only if they have good people working together towards well-understood goals. Understanding the spoken and unspoken needs and aspirations of employees allows an organisation the chance to come close to fulfilling the needs of clients and customers. This is where a design-thinking approach comes in. Following the design-thinking methodology allows leaders to arrive at project goals in a structured way. This becomes particularly important as workplace management instructions from top corporate management are often somewhat ill-defined. At the same time, the flexibility of the methodology allows multiple ideas to be tested.

Although there are many, we list down the top five benefits of adopting a design-thinking approach in workplace management:

Enhanced employee satisfaction: Design thinking places a strong emphasis on understanding the needs and preferences of end users. By incorporating user-centric solutions, workplace management teams can enhance employee satisfaction and create a workplace experience tailored to individual and team requirements.

Innovative problem-solving: Design thinking encourages a creative and iterative problem-solving process. This fosters innovation within the team, allowing them to generate novel solutions to workplace challenges and improve overall efficiency.

Adaptability to changing needs: The adaptive nature of design thinking aligns with the dynamic nature of workplace changes. By embracing a design-led approach, workplace management teams can respond effectively to evolving organisational needs, ensuring long-term success.

Collaborative team dynamics: Design thinking promotes interdisciplinary collaboration. When teams from FM, HR, IT and other departments collaborate in the problem-solving process, it fosters effective communication and coordination, breaking down silos and enhancing overall team dynamics.

Prevention of shortsighted solutions: Design thinking mitigates the risk of rushing to solutions without clearly defining the problems. By starting with a deep understanding of user needs, the approach ensures that workplace transformations are holistic, preventing shortsighted infrastructure plans and misalignments.

By embracing design thinking, workplace management teams can create an inclusive, adaptive and innovative environment that not only addresses immediate challenges but also contributes to the long-term success and satisfaction of employees within the organisation.

Ensure Roles Are Understood

Team members can meaningfully contribute to project goals if they are clear about their roles on the team set up to lead the transformation. Their roles within this team are often not the same as the one in their core function. It is the responsibility of the SPOC to ensure that everyone knows what they are expected to do within the team. This may seem obvious, but the reason this topic warrants a section is that we have seen so many teams fall apart because individual roles were not clear.

Team composition clarity: Even worse than role clarity is the fact that many teams have members who are not required on the team. Often, for political reasons or to not appear exclusionary, leaders include team members who really do not need to be on a team. So, they are there but not really there. These fence-sitting members will not be clear about their roles for the simple reason that they do not have a defined role in the team. For teamwork to be a success, a strong team leader will need to ensure they are free of political fuzziness. A team leader needs only those members who can contribute meaningfully to the purpose of the team.

Role clarity: Effective teamwork relies not only on a clear team composition but also on well-defined roles within the team. Instances abound where teams within organisations are structured haphazardly, leaving team members feeling underutilised and uncertain about their contributions. This lack of clarity can lead to team members either holding back their skills and creativity or unintentionally encroaching on each other's responsibilities. Avoiding such confusion and misunderstandings necessitates a precise definition of each member's role, ensuring that everyone understands their contributions and responsibilities within the team.

Coordination and structure: Members on a workplace management team are often experts. Although each member may be the best in their class, some all-star teams may underperform due to a lack of effective coordination. When not enough attention is paid to ensure smooth coordination, ineffectiveness ensues. A SPOC can ensure effective coordination by fostering open communication, implementing collaborative tools and promoting a positive team culture. Regular meetings, role clarity and a collaborative mindset contribute to streamlined efforts, preventing the underperformance that may arise from misaligned expertise within a workplace management team.

The shift to hybrid work has indeed introduced challenges in establishing effective structures within teams, especially when working virtually. In virtual settings, the absence of immediate, real-time cues can lead to communication gaps, reduced collaboration and unclear workflows. Establishing clear structures becomes crucial in a hybrid model to navigate these challenges, providing guidelines for communication, task distribution and collaboration. Structured frameworks become essential to maintain efficiency, foster teamwork and ensure a cohesive work environment amidst the flexibility of hybrid arrangements.

The familiarity fallacy: It is wrong to think that familiarity always breeds contempt. In organisations where team members know each other, they work better together. Familiarity fosters effective communication, trust and a shared understanding, leading to smoother teamwork. The existing relationships contribute to a positive team dynamic, enhancing overall productivity and synergy. So, there is much merit in having a few members who have known each other join a team together. Intuitively, we also believe that there should be at least one person who has not worked with the team on past projects. New team members bring fresh perspectives, innovative ideas and diverse skill sets. Their outsider viewpoint challenges groupthink, introduces novel approaches and stimulates creativity. The infusion of new talents enhances adaptability and broadens the team's problem-solving capabilities.

Remember the Five Steps

The designated team now needs to take action, and typically, their actions result in alterations to the workplace experience journey or its touchpoints. Before delving into the required actions, let's recall the five steps introduced earlier in the chapter titled 'The Employee as a Customer'.

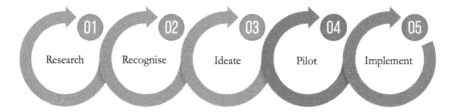

The subsequent sections of the book outline the key activities associated with each of these steps. For the reader's ease of understanding, the activities shown are for an assumed case of workplace transformation that involves a combination of new ways of working, new office designs and new digital workplace elements.

The Easy Work Question

In general, people opt for the easier path if given a choice. Delivery of personalised experiences based on past choices breeds familiarity, leading to easy adoption. Curation of such experiences relies on data-based decisions. The pages following this chapter describe key activities within the five critical steps in a workplace transformation initiative. Individual organisations may follow slightly different steps or refer to some of them with different names. However, in most cases, the high-level workflow of the five steps remains the same for all.

Whether organisations follow the steps as outlined here or a variant of this process, they will have the best chance of success if, at every step, leaders and participants are encouraged to ask: How might we make things easier and relatable so that employees can complete their tasks as effortlessly as possible? The moment this question is asked, the problem-solving process moves in a more positive direction.

The context of making things easy will vary from step to step and touchpoint to touchpoint.

One context can be that research to glean employee aspirations is an inherent part of any workplace transformation initiative. Amongst other methods, employee surveys are a common tool used to achieve this, but often faces low participation due to perceived complexity or lower priority. To boost response rates, adjustments can involve simplifying questionnaire formats, utilising user-friendly mobile forms, enhancing accessibility, offering incentives and providing gentle reminders. These adjustments not only ease the survey completion process but also foster higher engagement. By aligning research practices with the principle of making tasks more accessible, organisations can ensure valuable insights are gathered efficiently, contributing positively to the overall transformation journey.

The question of easy work needs to envelope all activities. For example, let us look at the design of a touchpoint, where an employee books a seat in the office via an employee app. Experience designers often define specific metrics for each touchpoint. For instance, a questionnaire or an interview surveying how employees use an app to find a seat within three seconds of accessing the app interface might include the following questions.

On a scale of 1 to 10,

- What is the degree to which the particular app can be used without much effort?
- What is the ability of the app to find desired information, what is the usefulness of the information provided and what is the credibility of the information provided?
- Would the user recommend the app to a colleague, and be happy using the app to get the desired information?
- Is navigation easy, well-organised and well-structured? Are layouts of seating options concise? Is it easy to understand the terms and conditions of booking seats and meeting rooms?
- Is it worth the effort needed to meet a goal using the app?
- Is it easier to use alternative routes to book a room than it is to use the app?
- Does using the app have a steep learning curve?
- What is the degree to which employees believe the app can lessen their efforts?
- Is the app user-friendly and less complicated to learn than any system or version of an app we have used before?

To be clear, we would never hand an employee a survey with the questions we just cited. Distributing such a survey isn't ideal. The complexity and nuanced nature of user experiences are better explored through interviews. During an interview, respondents, equipped with their smartphones, can engage in a more conversational and interactive dialogue with the interviewer. This approach ensures a deeper understanding of user sentiments and experiences, making it more effective than a traditional survey.

So, making work easy can be like a superpower for the workplace. Next, we're going to explore activities within the five steps to turn this superpower into reality. Think of these like a roadmap to make everyone's work life easier and more enjoyable. While each organisation might tweak the map slightly, the core essence remains constant, stemming from the question we've consistently urged leaders to ask: how can we make work easier to perform and relatable?

RESEARCH

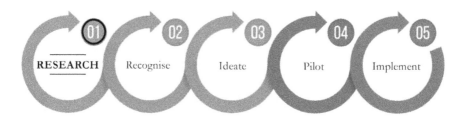

RESEARCH | Recognise | Ideate | Pilot | Implement

Collate Small Data

Any new initiative around work and workplaces involves the collection of small data (or people data) to understand business needs and user aspirations. When available, such data is complemented by big data or data thrown up by algorithm-based data-capturing sources, such as sensors or employee apps.

Once the goals of the workplace transformation initiative are clearly understood, it is time to collect people data.

Such data can be collected from a host of exercises like the following:

a) Employee surveys
b) Leadership interviews
c) Functional interviews
d) Focus groups
e) Observation studies
f) Infrastructure reviews

Employee Surveys

Mostly conducted through online forms, these surveys attempt to reveal user aspirations and needs. Usually questionnaire-based, they are aimed at generating a combination of qualitative and quantitative data. The design of such a survey needs to be aligned towards serving transformation goals—a simple design ensures a high response rate. Here are a few things to keep in mind:

- Be clear that the data collected serves one or more project goals
- Avoid asking for non-essential information
- Avoid leading questions and stick to closed questions that have multiple choice or checkbox-type answers
- Do not make the survey too long to complete; ideally it should be completed in less than six to seven minutes
- Think about incorporating an incentive into your survey, to elicit a higher response rate
- Create the survey so that employees can respond by smartphone or computer

Leadership Interviews

Workplace management task forces must hold one-on-one interviews with head office organisational leaders. Unless the group leader understands the top management's vision of how they want the organisation to proceed, no effective change can take place.

Determining which leaders to interview depends on the structure of the organisation. Irrespective of that, interviews should cover a section of the top management and a section of organisational vertical heads as well. Conversations help with securing insights about the position of leaders on certain topics, such as organisational vision, performance metrics, employee engagement, employee well-being, workplace culture and technology adoption. Although these interviews are very difficult to write about in abstract, any interview should address challenges and opportunities and what vision they have of the success of the transformation initiative.

Interviews need to be structured with a few icebreaker questions. The interviewer should give the organisational leader room in the conversation for ample scope to express their thoughts in a free-flowing manner. Generally, such interviews should be completed within one hour.

Functional Interviews

One-on-one interviews also need to be conducted with functional heads of departments who have a direct impact on the performance of the workplace. These include the HR head, FM head, CRE head, EHS (Employee Health & Safety) head and IT head.

The interviewer gains a targeted insight into each interviewee's perspective on current workplace challenges. The objective is to identify potential threats and concerns that organisational leaders may perceive in the context of a workplace transformation project.

These interviews need to be structured and to the point. Outlines or notes that look like a questionnaire should be drawn up, but not handed to the interviewee, as providing a predefined questionnaire may limit the spontaneity and depth of the interviewee's responses. The aim is to encourage open and candid discussions, allowing a more comprehensive understanding of the challenges and concerns in the workplace. The notes or outlines should be different for people in different disciplines. Although the primary interview needs to be covered within an hour, often it may become necessary to have follow-up sessions to understand particular areas of concern. Sometimes, the need for clarification may arise after a contrarian view emerges from some of the other interviews.

Focus Groups

These are group discussions or interviews to understand participants' perceptions of shared experiences of the workplace. They also help identify and explore how colleagues think and behave. During the focus groups, the facilitator should ask various what, why and how questions.

The focus group or groups should be made up of a small number of carefully selected people who participate in moderated discussions. Selection involves identifying individuals with insights into workplace dynamics and business needs, serving as eyes and ears on the ground, ensuring a diverse mix for valuable perspectives in discussions and exercises. Such groups are effective when they are structured around meticulously crafted interactive exercises that elicit often unspoken truths about the workplace and users. Of course, it is important as well to pick up the truths that are often spoken about within an organisation.

There are times when focus groups are found to be a good precursor to structured interviews. So, while leadership interviews and functional interviews are listed above focus groups in the order we have just provided, it may be useful at times to hold focus groups before these two types of interviews.

Multiple focus groups are usually conducted to cover the depth and breadth of the organisation. At least one focus group is recommended with potential change champions—individuals who volunteer or are nominated to facilitate change. They are often the people in an organisation who are most aware of what is happening at the ground level and understand the pulse of an entity.

Observation Studies

Observation studies are very effective when it comes to developing knowledge about aspects of a workplace that employees do not speak about or are unable to articulate. This process involves researchers observing the workplace either in-person or through photography or videography. A few critical areas that can be covered through such studies include:

- **Employee behaviour:** This can be understood by observing the ways physical and digital infrastructure are used. Watching employees at work on a typical day gives an observer information about how they behave in a variety of situations. Such knowledge, when collated, helps determine which behaviours need to be changed as part of a workplace transformation process.
- **Work patterns:** Employees have varying work patterns through the day. One may do focused work for two hours and then have meetings for three hours and travel to meet clients for the remaining hours. This changes day-to-day, and survey respondents cannot always accurately articulate this. Observations made by researchers during different times of the day and different days of the week help team leaders create productive workplace transformations.
- **Occupancy patterns:** Observations often reveal surprising data about the frequency and duration of employees' usage of different workspaces. For example, in the pre-COVID era, several organisations had dedicated desks for employees, but observation studies showed they were not occupied for more than 50 per cent of the time, due to work flexibility, frequent meetings, flexible work arrangements, project-based work and hot desking experiments. Conventionally

these studies were done manually, but today it is possible to generate data automatically when occupancy sensors are installed across the office.

Infrastructure Reviews

Reviews of existing physical and digital infrastructure are a must for team leaders to understand how an organisation uses its infrastructure. Physical infrastructure is made up of all buildings and associated services, including any automation. Digital infrastructure includes the buildings' IT, collaboration or meeting tools for hybrid/remote work, employee apps, seat booking apps and the integration of these with the physical infrastructure. Infrastructure reviews are specialised activities and must be undertaken by experts. They are usually conducted through a combination of on-site inspections and interviews with functional heads.

Balancing Internal and External Perspectives

While anyone with the relevant experience can complete these tasks, it has been seen that employees often do not share thoughts as freely with a researcher who is a colleague as opposed to an external researcher who is seen as a neutral party. Organisations often hire expert consultants because not only are they able to elicit relevant data but they also bring expertise without bias. They are also, at times, more adept at understanding industry trends. Independent consultants who specialise in workplace strategy are especially able to bring unbiased analysis and recommendations to the table.

Someone with experience from the internal team can of course lead the effort to pick the right mix of research projects and determine if they can be conducted internally or with external help. For both the external consultant and the internal team lead, it is pertinent to keep in mind the following:

Drawing impressions from raw data: Raw data, like the utilisation of work desks for 50 per cent of the time, is a starting point. The crucial step is interpreting what this implies for the workplace. Are there inefficiencies in space utilisation? Does it suggest a need for more flexible work arrangements or hot desking? Drawing meaningful insights requires translating numbers into actionable strategies.

Combining insights from different data sets: Each data set provides a piece of the puzzle. Combining data sets means looking beyond individual findings. For instance, correlating desk utilisation with employee feedback from surveys or observing how meeting room occupancy aligns with collaboration patterns. The synergy of these insights provides a comprehensive understanding, enriching the overall analysis.

Analysing small data in conjunction with big data: Small data, like individual survey responses, complements big data, such as analytics from workplace sensors or app usage. While small data captures nuances and individual experiences, big data offers broader trends. Integrating both ensures a holistic view. For instance, survey feedback on workspace preferences can align with big data indicating popular areas, refining strategies for optimal workplace design.

Essentially, a robust analysis extends beyond numbers, crafting a storyline that reveals significant implications, recognises patterns within various data sets and harnesses the advantages of both small and big data to attain comprehensive insights. The subsequent chapter delves into the realm of big data.

Collate Big Data

Big data refers to large volumes of data generated and transmitted from a wide variety of sources. It is characterised by three attributes:

- High volume, referring to the huge amount of data being generated
- High velocity, referring to the high speed at which data streams are generated and often processed and analysed
- High variety, referring to the different sources from which data is collected and the various forms this data takes

Traditional analytical tools are not equipped to handle this kind of complexity and volume. Specialised big data analytical software is used to manage such load.

In our day-to-day lives, data is constantly generated any time we open an app or search for something online or use our mobile devices to find directions while travelling. The result of this is a large collection of valuable information about our behaviours that companies love to analyse through algorithms. Such analysis is then used to curate personalised experiences for us. For example, when we search for a given product on the internet, we often receive an online advertisement for whatever we just searched, with the ad likely telling us that the product is being sold nearby at a particular store.

Another example involves Netflix. Every time you, assuming for the moment that you are a Netflix subscriber, watch something on the video streaming platform, the company collects data, such as the time at which you watched the show and whether you watched more than one episode. If you did watch more than one, Netflix keeps track of whether you watched them back-to-back or not. They also know if you paused in between and if you resumed after pausing.

The goal of collecting such information, and then automatically analysing it, is to offer you a high degree of personalisation. Netflix personalises by showing you clips from shows and movies that are similar to the ones you watch. Soon, they may use AI to create customised movie trailers for you. So if you like romantic movies, the trailer of a movie it shows you is likely to have more romantic scenes. This really is only the beginning. The degree to which personalisation can be taken knows no ends.

Data Sources at the Workplace

Since personalisation has become an intrinsic part of every aspect of life, employees are beginning to expect such experiences as they undertake their workplace journeys. For example, a very lucky employee could get accustomed to having a latte delivered to their cubicle at 3 p.m. each workday. No order would need to be placed. The digital systems would simply know.

As employees get used to personalised services in their day-to-day digital experiences, organisations will develop a corresponding ability to deliver curated workplace experiences to employees in their non-digital world, helping them fulfil their aspirations. As this happens, employee retention will improve.

However, one must tread carefully when dealing with data within organisations, as there are privacy issues. These stem from the fact that most of us do not like our every move tracked. Although the tools to collect all kinds of data about employees exist, most employees prefer that their employers involve themselves in a limited capacity where worker personal space is involved.

That said, most employees accept two broad categories of data collection sources: various types of sensors in the physical office and employee apps that help users plan and navigate their days in the workplace.

Organisations that have deployed solutions in these two categories get access to quite a bit of data around the following:

- Occupancy patterns
- Work styles
- A host of user choices around seating, commuting, eating, meeting and timing

Analysis of such data sets allows automated curation of user experiences ranging from recommended choice of desks and meeting rooms to temperature and lighting settings. The level of curation possible does not stop there, however. Let us broadly look at how sensors and employee apps add value to such curation.

Sensors

A wide variety of sensors can be installed within an office or at a campus. Popular sensors include:

- Temperature sensors
- Humidity sensors
- Light sensors
- Proximity sensors
- Motion/occupancy sensors
- Contact sensors
- Air quality sensors
- Electrical current monitoring sensors

These sensors record data that can be used in two broad ways, explained in greater detail in the paragraphs below: 1) to automate real-time changes to a workplace and 2) to initiate tactical workplace changes based on trend analysis.

Automated real-time changes: Sensors connected to the internet collect real-time data, which is then sent to data analysis software in the cloud. The software analyses this data and can be programmed to relay back an action to building services or to an employee user app. For example, a combination of light sensors and occupancy sensors in a meeting room, with a window to the outside, can track both the intensity of light in the meeting room and the occupancy. When two colleagues walk into the room for a meeting, the light intensity can be automatically adjusted based on the ambient light seeping in from the window. If the window has louvre blinds, the angle of the slats can be automatically turned to allow optimum light to enter the room. Artificial lighting may be turned on or off depending on a multitude of factors. Similarly, the heating or cooling in the room will be automatically adjusted. The sensing-analysis-action sequence happens within seconds, allowing a seamless experience for users. This is one of thousands of possible action options available within an office.

Tactical changes based on trend analysis: Sensors pick up data on a day-to-day basis. For example, one can clearly see for how long a six-person meeting room is used on average, see how frequently meetings are held, get to know various aspects about the power being consumed within the meeting room and so on. If these types of data can be collected for one meeting room, then every corner of the office can be tracked.

Over time, trends emerge about how the workplace is being used. This can help with determining what is working well and what is not. Insights from these trends are then used to make informed decisions and bring about improvements in the workplace. The ability to take data-driven decisions like this is what brings about efficiency in the workplace.

Employee Apps Connected to Workplace Management

As mentioned before, there are various tools used by employees that fit the workplace management theme: desk booking apps as well as apps that help employees navigate their way through workplace experience journeys, which collect data about user preferences. Such apps combine key features like:

- Booking desks and meeting rooms
- Planning and navigating commutes
- Ordering and managing food
- Integrating meeting and collaboration tools
- Keeping track of hygiene/cleaning/safety status of workspaces
- Recording attendance and other HR issues

The user can navigate all of the above and much more through an app. When developing such apps, it is important to ensure that data that may be considered private is not tracked. We are of the strong opinion that anything which tracks an employee's step-by-step movement is an infringement of privacy. However, when data related to something like personal choice of workspaces during work hours is captured, it helps curate personalised experiences for employees. For example, based on historical data trends, the app can prompt an employee by stating:

- 'You have been working from the office for the last three Tuesdays. Tomorrow is a Tuesday. Would you like to block a desk for tomorrow?'
- 'There is a meeting scheduled with Paul in your calendar at 2 p.m. on Monday. Would you like a small meeting room to be booked in the office?'

Analysing Employee App Data in Combination with Sensor Data

The ability to analyse employee app data in combination with sensor data enables organisations to generate good experiences for employees and help them avoid bad ones. The combination of app and sensor data also facilitates analysis of certain situations. For example, sensors may show that employees turn up late for their individual meetings on Fridays after some of them book group meeting rooms for this day. It is also recorded, through their own apps, that the cleaners are much busier cleaning these meeting rooms on Fridays. In addition, the sensors that monitor occupancy of these spaces, without tracking which employee is using them, show that some meetings begin late after the previous one ended on time. These data points also reveal that one person comes into the room and leaves before the next group enters the room. One can see that these two ways of collecting data create an ability to very accurately predict trends.

Gap analysis helps with figuring out the root cause of the problem. In this case, it is concluded that Fridays lead to more mini-parties in the meeting rooms starting at lunchtime. Furthermore, through interviews, it is concluded that the single individuals entering the rooms after one group leaves and before another enters are the cleaners. They come in at a rate that is three times higher on Fridays than on other days. Whether an organisation wants to address this issue is another matter. But by combining data sets and doing a form of gap analysis, it is possible to understand problems. The organisation might want to put a fifteen-minute break period between meetings starting at noon on Fridays or later to allow a cleaner to enter the meeting rooms and clean them when needed.

When amalgamated, data from sensors and employee apps

becomes a powerful tool for organisations, enabling them to make informed decisions, recognise patterns and iteratively enhance the workplace environment, fostering improved efficiency and heightened employee satisfaction. During the research phase of a workplace transformation initiative, the potency of trend analysis is accentuated, especially for organisations equipped with historical data from sensors and/or employee apps. The reliability of big data often surpasses that of small data, positioning it as a robust resource. The insights derived from the amalgamation of big and small data prove instrumental in optimising employee experiences and proactively addressing challenges. This holistic approach to data analysis becomes a cornerstone for organisations striving for continual improvement and innovation in their workplace strategies.

RECOGNISE

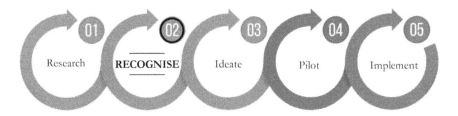

01 Research   **02 RECOGNISE**   03 Ideate   04 Pilot   05 Implement

Draw Insights from Data

According to technology experts at the research and consulting company Forrester Research, Inc., 74 per cent of companies want to be 'data-driven', but only 29 per cent are successful at connecting analytics to action. Going forward, organisations will become more data-driven, especially when it comes to understanding their employees. Most of the effort behind a data-driven approach so far has been largely around understanding customers, enabling higher sales of products and services. Post the COVID-19 pandemic, however, there has been heightened interest in caring for employees and this has opened the floodgates for data-driven decision-making when it comes to fulfilling their needs and aspirations.[56]

Commit to Analytics

If the techniques discussed earlier are deployed, a great amount of data related to employees and their workplace practices can be collected. However, raw data is meaningless. Data becomes powerful when knowledge is drawn from it, patterns appear, tactics to bring greater efficiency become apparent and actionable steps are determined. While signing up for new-age tools such as employee apps and sensors, it is important to make a strong commitment to data analytics so that informed decisions can be made based on the analysis. We have seen managers in organisations getting very excited by some of these new tools and investing in them enthusiastically. While they can help fulfil some utilitarian needs like the ability to book seats, parking spots, etc., there is far greater value that can be derived from them. This value lies in the trends that emerge from analysing the collected data, which helps make data-driven decisions for the future. Some of the analytics can be provided as standard offerings by suppliers, but it is important to ask for what one needs. And what one needs depends on the transformation goals.

What Are Insights?

Imagine a pyramid with three levels. The bottom-most level comprises data. This could be, for example, raw numbers that might come from surveys. The next level of the pyramid is information. This is data that has been processed and easier to understand than raw data. An example of this is the output that appears on the dashboard attached to an employee app software package. These apps generate graphs and pie charts tracking trends, to which HR managers have access. The dashboard makes it easier for the manager to consume all the data collected in a way that makes information valuable.

The top level of the pyramid is insights. Insights are developed when researchers consume the information and create hypotheses, make observations, draw conclusions and come up with possible suggestions. Suggestions are the beginning of the journey towards taking hypotheses-based action. When it comes to workplace transformation, these are the steps towards arriving at a workplace strategy.

A very particular example is in order. Let's say that an employee survey shows the following information: 80 per cent of employees do not like to work from offices on Mondays. This information is useless unless we can arrive at a conclusion about why employees feel this way. There could be multiple hypotheses about why this is: heavy traffic on Mondays or people preferring longer weekends. There might be another ten reasons why employees do not like to come to the office on Mondays. To test these hypotheses, a researcher may look at supplementary data from a focus group. This data could help managers arrive at a conclusion about what the main drivers concerning Mondays are. Hypothetically, let's assume that further research helps management conclude that the sole reason that makes Mondays a bad day to come to the office is that employees prefer extended weekends.

This is now an insight, which may be actionable on its own or in combination with other insights. In the case of Mondays, an actionable policy might be to move to a four-day work week or to keep the office shut on Mondays. You can see how the hypothetical data might indicate such a policy change.

For every piece of decisive information derived about the workplace, get into the habit of asking: What does it mean for the workplace?

Deriving Insights from Human Interaction:
The Dell Interview

Insights are drawn not only from statistical data but also from non-statistical data, usually derived from human interaction. We would like to cite the example of one such interaction. One of us used to work with a former CEO of Dell, the technology giant. One of us also knows Seth, a computer scientist who currently works for Dell. We have discussed and shared learnings about business management. In a recent interaction with Seth, he spoke about a big online meeting with colleagues in which, amongst others, his boss and his boss's boss were present. They were discussing issues around employee well-being. Dell, for many years, has been known and admired for its caring attitude towards its employees and flexibility around work hours and days. Employees stick around for the perceived benefits, even though the pay offered may not be always be the highest amongst competitors.

In the meeting, Seth's boss said, in the presence of his boss, that he knows that his well-being is 'out of whack' when he is unable to exercise three days a week. He was referring to times when work pressure leaves him with no time or motivation to go to the gym. This single statement makes for an interesting study, allowing us to derive insights about the culture present within Dell at the time.

Overcoming the fear factor: Seth's boss felt secure about opening up in front of his boss, as well as in front of his subordinates, about how work pressure could be damaging to his overall well-being. The ability to speak openly like this, without fear of being judged, indicates a positive culture at Dell. It seems that speaking up is rewarded, not punished.

Employees often do not speak up because they are introverted or because the inherent culture of an organisation causes social exclusion or perceived punishment when they speak up or challenge norms. Companies have much to benefit from when employees feel comfortable about candidly voicing their opinions, suggestions or concerns. Speaking up often promotes innovation, referred to as the secret sauce of business success. Innovation, however, needs diversity of thought and action and a culture in which people can be open about their opinions.

In environments that encourage open expression, creativity, problem-solving and adaptability flourish, thereby enhancing teamwork, employee engagement and overall organisational resilience. Moreover, organisations become better at handling threats when the on-ground pulse is visible and noticed.

Well-being is an individual thing: Seth's boss felt that a minimum of three days of exercise was very important for his own sense of well-being. For someone else within Dell, it may be something else, like the ability to get a certain amount of time with family or the ability to go on vacations at certain frequencies. Taking a cookie-cutter approach to employee well-being does not work. Life is different for different individuals. Mandating that everyone does yoga twice a week may be well-meaning, but is unlikely to work. Instead, organisations should offer a variety of options to employees to choose from.

Practise what you preach: Organisations sometimes resort to sloganeering—for example, 'We encourage free speech'. Often, when we hear this, we notice that the words are not followed by actions. Similarly, one often comes across HR messaging around how companies 'care for employee health'. Again, we compare words to actions. When we see adequate facilities like gyms, yoga rooms and walking tracks that are paid for by the company, then we know they are serious. Unless there is a culture in which people are not castigated for doing things like going to the gym three times a week, attempts at building a culture in which health is prioritised will fail. Sloganeering or kind-sounding HR policies are not enough. Talk needs to followed by written policies and actions that build a culture in which employees can exercise and be healthy.

Lead by example: Seth's boss speaking out in front of his superior and juniors is an example of both free speech and leading by example. He was sending out a message about how important exercise was for employee well-being. Leading by example is a leadership style where you model the behaviour you want to see in your team members. When you do so, you don't just push team members towards excellence—rather, you actively demonstrate that excellence.

The insights derived from a candid remark like the one by Seth's boss about the importance of exercise, when examined in conjunction with other research data sets gathered from interviews, focus groups and data collected from employee apps or sensor data, can offer a comprehensive understanding of the prevailing culture within an organisation. In this case, the open and non judgmental environment that encourages such disclosures reflects positively on the company's ethos. This nuanced information, when integrated with qualitative and quantitative findings from various sources, can illuminate a broader issue beyond individual exercise preferences. By delving into diverse data sets, organisations can pinpoint underlying challenges related to employee well-being, engagement and innovation. This multifaceted approach ensures a clear and holistic definition of the problem, laying the foundation for thoughtful and effective solutions that address the root causes.

Define the Problem Correctly

'If I were given one hour to save the planet, I would spend 59
minutes defining the problem and one minute resolving it.'
—Albert Einstein

Workplace transformation projects are initiated to achieve certain
goals that relate to existing challenges and problems. Having very
particular goals helps a transformation team define problems
correctly. It is pivotal that problems be defined accurately because
otherwise transformation initiatives run the risk of missing their
goals by solving the wrong problems. Problem diagnosis is equally,
if not more, important than problem-solving. Often, enthused by a
penchant for action, managers tend to switch quickly into solution
mode without fully understanding the problems that require fixing.
Sometimes such issues grow out of teams understanding situations
from a narrow or incorrect perspective. Research and knowledge
development provide opportunities to look at issues from different
perspectives.

Reframe the Problem

When managers go into solution mode without clearly defining
the problem, symptoms that indicate a festering issue often don't
go away. If applying Band-Aids on the symptoms does not resolve
the issue, it is best to step back from the problem and look at it
through new lenses or a different perspective. Better still, avoid the
urge to jump to solutions before clearly understanding what you
need to solve. Get into the habit of reframing.

In the earlier chapter on persuasive design, we wrote about the
manager who got over the frustration of poor response rates to
employee surveys by changing the data-collection method. Instead

of spending too much time trying to come up with the best ways to improve survey response, she decided to draw from data that was already being collected through an employee app and sensors in the office. All that was required was her making minor tweaks in the measurement parameters.

The original problem she was dealing with was 'poor response rate to employee surveys'. When she reframed the problem, it turned into 'difficulty in getting reliable and accurate data to measure on-the-ground pulse'. This opened up a whole universe of new ways to solve the problem. She also found out later that the new way of solving the problem, drawing from employee app and sensor data, turned out to be more reliable and actionable. We sense this was probably because, historically, survey responses may have reflected what respondents felt was the right thing to say, whereas data collected via apps and sensors revealed the truth.

To make this example more relevant to this book, we would like to propose to readers the 'so what' approach. If the simple understanding of the problem is 'survey response rate is poor', ask: So what? By doing this, a company may find that the 'because' answer is very helpful. So, for example, if the response to the 'so what?' question about response rates is 'Because we have to obtain reliable data about hybrid work policies', the action to be taken doesn't have to be about surveys. The real problem was an inability to get reliable and accurate data. Once the manager realised there was a different problem to solve, she could go about using sensors and other means to collect much of the data she was trying to obtain. When the problem was reframed to 'inability to get reliable and accurate data', it was not difficult to see that the solution was right there. The original framing of the problem was not necessarily wrong. The manager could have found value by asking employees to fill out another long survey, even if they resented being asked. But by analysing the situation and reframing the problem, she realised there was an easier problem to solve. The very notion of a single root cause to the problem was misleading.

We have seen managers asking the question 'so what' five times in succession when trying to solve a problem. They did this to discover whether problems were different from what they thought they were. When the 'so what' question is asked the right number of times, the solution usually pops up more quickly.

Defining the problem correctly often leads to unexpected radical improvements. Sometimes teams can find fixes for issues that have plagued an organisation for years.

Think Like a Doctor

When it comes to figuring out problems, think about how doctors work. Doctors do a bunch of tests to understand what's wrong with a patient. Similarly, managers should carefully look at the issues their teams bring up. They need to break down these problems into smaller parts, making it easier to understand. This breaking down process is called analysis. After that, they need to put these parts together in a creative way, like solving a puzzle; this is called synthesis. The key is to organise, understand and put the information into context to define the problem accurately. Imagine it as a complex dance between taking things apart and putting them back together. This process helps the real problem become clear. Without a clear understanding of the problem, finding effective solutions is only half-done.

IDEATE

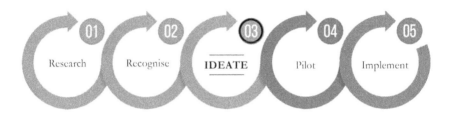

Research Recognise **IDEATE** Pilot Implement

Establish Strategy Direction

The process of defining a problem correctly is significantly enriched through the synthesis and analysis of diverse data sets gathered from various sources. By carefully examining and combining this information, a nuanced understanding of the problem emerges. Subsequently, employing ideation techniques such as brainstorming, storyboarding, mind mapping and reverse thinking becomes instrumental in navigating through potential solutions for the accurately identified problem. These creative approaches foster a dynamic environment in which innovative ideas can flourish and contribute to problem-solving. However, it's crucial to note that the effectiveness of the ideation process is heightened when it culminates in the formulation of a well-documented workplace strategy. From an organisational perspective, this strategy serves as a tangible roadmap, outlining the identified problem, proposed solutions and a systematic plan of action. A documentable strategy not only facilitates clear communication but also provides a structured framework for the implementation of solutions, ensuring coherence and alignment with overarching organisational goals and objectives.

Workplace strategy involves the dynamic alignment of an organisation's work patterns within the work environment to enable peak performance and reduce costs.

A workplace strategy is not often written up in the same way a corporate or NGO strategy document might be composed. Instead, such documents are usually reports that collate information, reach some conclusions about the past and suggest a way forward for the future. These reports are written in an easy-to-understand manner, and focus on goals and patterns and mention any special initiatives that have been identified. A data-driven approach to write-ups gives organisational leaders a sense that those in charge of workplace management have moved beyond the ideation stage and have formulated a strategy.

Attributes of reports that might establish a sense of seriousness include the following:

- Framework for hybrid work policies
- Real estate portfolio assessments
- Move or stay decisions
- Basis for office layout changes, if necessary
- Descriptions of alignment of leadership vision and user aspirations
- Blueprints for future ways to work

A Report with Recommendations for Major Change

A workplace strategy report that describes transformation plans is usually the result of hundreds of hours of research, analysis and ideation. While the body of a report might be fairly short, the annexes of such a report often run into hundreds of pages. The summarised version of such a report must contain at least the following basic chapters:

- The context or the story behind the initiative identified
- The goals
- Research methodology and activities
- Ideation process and findings
- Analysis
- Conclusions and recommendations

The conclusions and recommendations need to be focused on transformation goals and need to be as precise as possible. For example, if the primary goal is enhancing hybrid models of work, a good report ought to cite specifics such as:

- As much as 27 per cent of the sales team to work remotely on a regular basis
- When the sales team is in the office, they will need access to desks for 55 per cent of the time
- Employees can be allowed to work remotely two days per week, with either Monday or Friday as a mandatory day in office

When specific recommendations are backed up by data, it becomes easy for policymakers to roll out evidence-based policies and for design and project briefs to be clear.

It Is an Integrative Process

Once regular reports are submitted and transformation studies are complete, the strategy-setting process can begin. This process varies greatly based on the transformation needed. However, once marching orders are understood by all stakeholders involved, action can be taken. Depending on the conclusions and recommendations in such reports, organisations usually set in motion the right teams and consultants to act upon those suggestions. For example, if there is a recommendation to change office layouts, organisations will hire an interior designer and a project manager to get the work done. If there is a recommendation to consolidate the real estate portfolio and co-locate, an organisation is most likely to appoint a real estate agent to action this. Most entities are well set up to take action after recommendations are made.

Using Consultants

Conventionally, the steps leading up to major workplace strategy reports that go beyond logistics have been largely driven by workplace strategy consultants. Experience indicates, though, that establishing a strategy should not be viewed as an external consultant's job in its entirety. An integrative process requires active internal participation from day one. An external consultant can only guide and provide the framework for ideation to roll forward and for strategy to emerge. Not even the best workplace strategists can establish a strategy for an organisation without active participation from internal stakeholders.

The steps leading up to an integrative workplace strategy report are best traversed together. Over time, consultants and internal stakeholders work together as one team to validate findings. The involvement of internal stakeholders is even more extensive in the case of an important intervention, such as framing a new policy for remote work.

Having no involvement with the internal stakeholder often leads to reports that merely gather dust, with no one invested in their implementation. When external consultants co-create the strategy with internal stakeholders, implementation is usually achieved more easily.

The conclusions and recommendations articulated in workplace strategy reports do not invariably advocate sweeping transformations; rather, they may encompass a spectrum of suggestions or even endorse maintaining existing structures. In certain instances, the advice offered might advocate the preservation of all facilities precisely as they stand. While this directive may entail minimal immediate action items for FM, CRE and IT teams, it underscores the nuanced nature of strategic guidance. It is imperative to recognise that in the contemporary landscape characterised by volatility, instances where maintaining the status quo is advised are relatively infrequent. By embracing flexibility and actively engaging with the ever-changing landscape, organisations can effectively navigate the complexities of workplace strategy, responding proactively to emerging challenges and opportunities.

Take an Integrated Approach to Workplace Design

A workplace strategy report might encompass recommendations concerning an organisation's office real estate portfolio. Typically, the CRE team within most organisations is tasked with managing the suggested changes in real estate portfolios. These recommendations address a range of issues, such as:

- Where to locate new offices
- Where to retain existing offices
- Where to expand or shrink offices

A CRE leader working on these issues usually requires the help of external consultants. These consultants have traditionally been one of two types: those who negotiate with landlords/sellers, or those who design and conduct test fits of shortlisted options and/ or analyse the best fit for the organisation's needs within each of the options.

Changes in Office Design

A workplace strategy report might also propose alterations to the design of office spaces. Changes could include any or a combination of the following:

Change in design philosophy: An organisation may want offices to be designed for resilience or agility rather than efficiency or productivity.

Change in the type of workspaces within an office: An organisation with three types of work seats could move to provide a wider variety of seating options.

Change in some of the design standards to meet aesthetic or utilitarian needs: Aesthetic changes may be required due to alterations in the brand identity or for other special purposes. Utilitarian changes may include reforms in the size or shape of workspaces, such as increasing the size of desks or providing height-adjustable desks.

In most organisations, the CRE team, with support from the FM team, usually leads these parts of workplace design. However, these days, office design is no longer done in a silo. It needs active coordination and participation from HR and IT leaders. External help is also usually called for. What follows is a combined list of two consultant-related themes. In each bullet is both the category of consultant that might be needed and a short description of the consultant's role:

- Interior designers and/or architects to pull together the spatial changes
- MEP (mechanical, engineering and plumbing) consultant to support the spatial changes with the right building services
- Green consultant to enable sustainability or to secure any certification required
- Project manager to coordinate and manage the fit-out process, budgets and timelines
- Workplace strategist to monitor translation of strategy to office design

In your upcoming workplace transformation project involving redesign, architects, interior designers, MEP consultants and green consultants may work collaboratively, integrating their contributions seamlessly through the use of AI.

Use of AI in Office Design

The way office spaces are designed is undergoing a radical transformation, driven by the innovative power of generative AI. As a reminder, generative AI employs algorithms to independently produce fresh and distinctive content—whether images, text or designs—drawing from patterns and data it has been trained on. These AI tools are not mere design assistants; they are co-creators, partnering with architects, designers and MEP consultants to craft optimised and inspiring work environments.

AI analyses vast data, from building codes to employee preferences, to generate layouts that are efficient, functional and beautiful. Imagine AI suggesting a focus room based on real-time noise or advising desk arrangements for better collaboration.

But AI's impact extends beyond practicality. It champions sustainability, ensuring climate-resilient buildings that are not only visually stunning but also environmentally conscious and prepared for future challenges. AI simulates various conditions and predicts climate change impacts, enabling the design of resilient infrastructure. However, AI isn't here to replace human creativity. It is a powerful collaborator, providing data for human designers to translate into beautiful and functional spaces. The best results come from a harmonious blend of both.

This revolution is fuelled by innovative tools like:

- Concept Design Exploration: Tools like Midjourney spark initial ideas with stunning renders, while ARCHITEChTURES and Ark AI explore layouts and optimise designs.
- Automated Design Generation: Maket.ai crafts floorplans in seconds, Sloyd.AI designs custom furniture and NodeBox empowers exploration with visual programming.

- Optimisation and Sustainability: Autodesk Forma evaluates environmental impact, and BricsCAD BIM automates tasks, freeing up valuable time for creative thinking.

Building Management Systems and Automation Changes

Traditionally, building management systems (BMS) were used to manage building efficiency as well as fire and security systems. The ability to manage and monitor all mechanical and electrical equipment such as ventilation, lighting, power systems, fire systems and security systems in an integrative manner through computer-based applications led to the birth of integrated building management systems (IBMS). Now, with the advent of IoT and AI, it is possible to manage such systems through apps. AI applications have empowered IBMS to enhance building efficiency, automation and sustainability. Machine learning algorithms analyse data from various sensors, optimising energy usage, predictive maintenance and security protocols. This evolution in IBMS leverages real-time insights, enabling proactive decision-making for building operations. AI driven features like predictive analytics, occupant behaviour analysis and adaptive climate control have elevated IBMS to an intelligent, responsive system. The marriage of AI with IBMS not only ensures streamlined building management but also sets the stage for smart, energy-efficient and responsive infrastructures.

As a result, IBMS is no more just a technological concept—it has completely changed how some employees function. While this is true at the facilities management level, hyper-connectivity and the possibility of automating building systems have also opened up tremendous opportunities to curate employee experiences.

Advanced automation results in IT teams working hand-in-hand with FM teams. HR's role in these changes is becoming more and more important as organisations strive to bring about smoother curated experiences for employees as they navigate a day at work.

Improvements and Upgrades in Collaboration Technology

Years ago, in 2006, IT leader Cisco launched Telepresence, a bouquet of products designed to link two physically separated rooms so they resemble a single conference room, regardless of location. One of us was part of the team setting up a Telepresence room at a client location at the time. What was amazing was that when you sat down for a meeting with people on the screens, it felt like everyone was in the same room. Setting up such rooms was a relatively expensive proposition, and Telepresence remained a niche product for many years.

Setting up a Telepresence room involved designing every inch of the room to the smallest detail, including the lighting and the furniture, to bring together a life-like experience of talking to colleagues remotely. This was an early experience of how physical objects in spaces worked in an integrated manner with a digital medium.

With hybrid work becoming the norm and employees working regularly on a remote basis, the need to connect physical spaces with digital spaces has increased. Individuals within organisations are quickly moving back and forth from a) device to device, and b) virtual audiovisual communication to face-to-face interactions. The acceleration to working in the metaverse will only boost the need for creating physical spaces that can connect remote colleagues seamlessly, wherever they are located.

When workplace strategists make recommendations regarding this type of integration, the workplace management team usually looks for external assistance from collaboration tech suppliers such as Cisco or Zoom, which integrate their online tools with physical spaces. Or they look to interior designers and support from MEP consultants to integrate solutions. The demand for professionals capable of bridging the gap between physical and digital realms underscores the importance of individuals who possess the skills to seamlessly integrate both. Workplace management teams must adeptly coordinate and integrate the services offered by interior designers, MEP consultants and technology suppliers responsible for establishing digital workspaces.

Redesign of Policies Around New Ways of Working

The COVID experience saw a lot of organisations determine new work policies, called 'agile/hybrid work policy'. Some organisations went the extra mile and produced additional playbooks for new ways of working. Writing these user manuals for the new workplace requires a deep understanding of the discipline of human resources as well as an understanding of the physical and the hybrid office. Policies like these work as frameworks of the dos and don'ts of working in a hybrid environment. Policies cannot cover all aspects of work in the hybrid environment partly because everything is in a constant state of flux.

Drafting a new policy of this type is an internal matter and is often led by the HR department. However, they can seek help from change management experts who do everything from providing boilerplate language for policies to facilitating team workshops meant to provide clarity about new workplace arrangements.

It's All Connected

All of the above is interconnected. Workplace design needs to be looked at as a web where design and management interact. The evolving landscape, where physical and digital realms merge, propels workplace management into a central role. This discipline takes the lead as organisations seamlessly integrate physical and digital aspects. The interplay between design philosophy, technology and policy underscores the holistic approach required to create a harmonious work environment. As workplaces evolve into hybrid spaces, the orchestration of these interconnected facets becomes paramount, with workplace management leading the charge towards a cohesive and integrated future.

PILOT

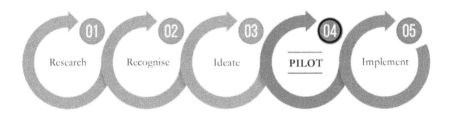

01 Research 02 Recognise 03 Ideate 04 **PILOT** 05 Implement

Pilot the Workplace Transformation

Workplace transformation initiatives ought to be piloted first within a part of the organisation or within a part of an office before being rolled out to the whole office. Changes, if any, need to be tested through a pilot. Lessons learnt from pilots become legends around organisations. Ignoring the value of pilots in the workplace management world has led to the loss of a job for more than one leader. Managers must accept that it makes sense to make mistakes in pilots, then improve the offering, pilot again and only then roll out an initiative across the board.

The fact that what we are saying is so well-documented and still ignored by so many encourages us to continue. No one wants to invest tonnes of money in a full roll-out and risk failure. Whether one is planning a new piece of automation involving sensors or a new office layout, it makes sense to try something small first.

Pilots help organisations test out solutions and gain confidence before fully implementing them. Let's take the example of implementing a new collaborative workspace. Before rolling out the new workspace design across the entire organisation, you can pilot a small section or department. Set up the new collaborative environment, complete with the intended furniture, technology and layout changes. Allow employees in that pilot area to work in this transformed space for a specific trial period. This pilot phase helps assess how well the new workspace fosters collaboration, improves workflow and enhances employee satisfaction. Collect feedback from the employees in the pilot to identify any adjustments needed before implementing the changes organisation-wide or across the entire office. Piloting allows you to test and refine the transformation on a smaller scale, ensuring that the broader implementation is more likely to succeed and meet the overall project goals.

However, with hybrid work at play, and with the discipline of workplace management involving multiple departments, things get complex at times, due to the intricate interplay of various departments. Hybrid work introduces additional layers of intricacy, requiring collaboration and coordination among diverse teams. To ensure robust pilots, we have an approach we would like to suggest that puts prototyping before pilots.

Prototype First, Then Pilot

A prototype is an early version of a solution and can be used in relation to products or services. Prototypes are working models, usually meant for internal testing. They normally encompass all the intended functionalities. Prototypes not only give shape and tangibility to an idea but also help the team identify problems early on. The team goes back to the drawing board, multiple times if required, to iron out problems that prototypes throw up. In the context of this book, we refer to pilots as trying out a workplace transformation initiative in one location or one part of a workplace, before rolling it out across the organisation. And by prototyping, we refer to testing the individual parts of the pilot throughout the journey to piloting. Prototyping is not about testing an entire suite of services or products—only the critical aspects.

Some of the main advantages of prototyping are that they

- Help save time and money
- Provide data for the documentation of a project
- Give an opportunity for team members to work on a tangible product, which helps generate more ideas and improve solutions
- Allow implementation issues to be examined before a full roll-out
- Bring out shortcomings in a way that leads to less embarrassment for the organisation
- Add to securing the initial buy-in from all the required players before a pilot or a roll-out can be successful

Once organisations become accustomed to prototyping, they rarely abandon the practice.

To take an example from the field of work, if you are conducting an employee survey to gather data, ask for a prototype of the survey form. Test it out internally, with one question, to see how the form behaves, how the responses are captured and if you are receiving the data you need to help meet project goals. If your survey is going to be conducted online, test it out on multiple devices (mobile phones and computers) and see how convenient it is and how much time it takes to complete the one question. Use the whole survey in a pilot once it is prototyped. And then use the survey broadly only when you are convinced it is fit for the intended purpose.

Another example of a prototype is testing the implementation of flexible work hours. Before rolling out a policy that covers flexible work hours, create a prototype that outlines the proposed flexible work schedule. Test it with a small group of employees, allowing them to follow the suggested flexible hours for a trial period. During this prototype phase, assess the impact on productivity, collaboration and employee satisfaction. Gather feedback on the feasibility and effectiveness of the proposed flexible work hours. Adjust the prototype based on the insights gained and then pilot the refined flexible work schedule with a larger group. This staged approach ensures that the organisation can fine-tune its hybrid work policies before implementing them on a broader scale, fostering a smoother transition and increased chances of meeting the needs of employees.

Once you embrace the habit of prototyping, the possibilities for enhancing every facet of the emerging hybrid workplace are boundless. From flexible schedules to collaboration tools, workspace designs, communication channels and beyond, the potential for improvement is vast. Here is a brief but not exhaustive list of things we frequently observe undergoing the prototyping process:

- Interviews
- Employee apps
- Layouts
- Fit-out components like furniture and fixtures
- Workshops
- Change management bulletins
- Digital info-packs for new ways of working

Cultivating a Prototyping Culture

Altering the prototyping speed allows a diverse set of practices to be formed around the amount of testing that the entirety of a specific solution or idea needs. For example, teams can do rapid prototyping during any stage of the solution development cycle for any components or sub-components of a project. Rapid prototyping is about creating a prototype quickly to visually and functionally evaluate a part or parts. Sometimes, individual parts are rapidly created separately and assembled to test the product prototype. For example, if one wants to rapid-prototype the outline for a leadership interview, they can quickly initiate a role-play format to test it. Developing a culture of prototyping de-risks project stakeholders as organisations move towards new ways of working. A culture of prototyping can lead to robust pilots.

Manage the Change

Any change resulting out of a workplace strategy planning programme—following a detailed plan—has to be timed correctly. A commitment to go down the path of workplace transformation is a commitment to do something good for an organisation's employees, and that cannot be easily aborted halfway through the process. However, even when workplace transformation programmes are well-timed and well-planned, it has to be acknowledged that sometimes they fail as employees and/or managers reject them.

Expect Resistance to Change

When encountering resistance to workplace transformation initiatives, it is crucial to understand that human nature often inclines individuals to resist change, particularly in the initial stages, when the unknown looms large. The familiarity of routine and the known environment provide a sense of security, and deviations from this norm can trigger a primal fear response. This resistance is not necessarily a sign of stubbornness or unwillingness to embrace improvement; rather, it reflects deeply rooted survival instincts. Recognising and understanding this natural resistance is key to navigating change effectively, as it allows a more empathetic approach to introducing new ideas or practices.

For instance, a company introducing a 'mandatory three days in office' policy may face pushback from employees accustomed to non-mandatory routines. Acknowledging this resistance, the organisation can implement change management strategies, such as communication campaigns, workshops or gradual phase-ins, to foster understanding and alignment. Embracing resistance as part of the change process enables organisations to navigate challenges more effectively and ensure successful transformations.

Let us look at an example of how managers can react to change in the workplace. A move to an agile work style may mean that an organisation does away with private offices. Organisations can instead introduce workspaces that leaders can sign up for and work out of. Despite the collective decision-making process, some managers may perceive the shift as a loss of entitlement earned through years of hard work, triggering feelings of resentment or being snubbed. To navigate this change effectively, communication becomes paramount. Ensuring transparent and inclusive communication about the rationale behind the shift, emphasising the benefits for both individuals and the organisation, can alleviate concerns. Additionally, providing a platform for managers to express their feelings, acknowledging their contributions and involving them in the implementation process fosters a sense of inclusion. Implementing change gradually, offering support mechanisms and showcasing success stories from early adopters can further mitigate resistance and pave the way for a smoother transition.

A well-crafted change management initiative can prevent the worst from happening and is a necessity for workplace transformation initiatives. At the risk of being redundant, it is important to have a plan in place before transforming workplaces.

Empathy and Change Champions

As mentioned earlier, empathy has to be at the core of any workplace transformation. Empathy, in the context of this book, involves developing a deep understanding of the needs and aspirations of the people for whom one is trying to develop new ways of working.

Change champions are individuals within an organisation who are nominated or selected or those who volunteer to facilitate change. They are the eyes and ears on the ground and usually have a good sense of the pulse within their teams. Generally, a group of change champions is selected early on when a workplace transformation initiative begins, and they stay involved throughout the various stages, all the way through implementation. These champions need to be picked in such a manner that the group is representative of the depth and breadth of the organisation. They can be from any level within the organisation—the best results are seen when different levels are well represented.

While gathering people data, at least one focus group workshop should be held with the change champions. This group will help researchers secure very good knowledge about the pulse on the ground. Later, as the initiative makes progress, change champions become instrumental in instituting change, advocating for it on a day-to-day basis and promoting the change from within. Their advocacy may be both formal and informal, occurring through casual conversations, socialising the change with colleagues and subtly promoting it without making others feel like they are being preached to. They are seen as the key communicators of the change and work to de-escalate conflict when necessary. They promote new ideas for change in the early days and motivate others to share in this experience. They are the driving force of organisational change.

Change Communication Plan

Communicating change in a way that all levels of employees can understand and accept is not easy and requires a change communication plan. The plan is a roadmap of all the activities surrounding a transformation campaign and should include detailed information about different channels for communication that have been identified. A good change communication plan ought to cover the following:

- Different types of activities
- Frequency and dates
- Audience
- Owner, who is responsible for the particular activity
- Agent, who will be the one to deliver the activity
- Channel to be used for the delivery (email, townhall, microsite, etc.)
- Key messaging
- Preparation required for the activity
- Post activity follow-up required

Engaging Employees

The essence of a human-centric approach is that employees feel their voices are heard when they are involved at some level in a transformation process. While every process is different, almost all workplace transformation plans have room for employee involvement. We can't emphasise this strongly enough. There can be problems even when employees are engaged, but it greatly increases the chances of the success of the transformation, as the resistance and issues reduce.

It might be useful to examine briefly why employee engagement works. On a very basic level, co-creating is better than having an individual invent every new policy. When people feel that they are part of the team that created something, a sense of ownership kicks in and an emotional buy-in is initiated. Emotional buy-ins towards change are just as important as logical buy-ins. An HR manager may give a long talk about the logic behind instituting change, and the logic may be very sound, but without the emotional buy-in, no amount of logical reasoning will work. Employee participation helps generate that emotional buy-in.

Further, change champions stay engaged through the entirety of the process. They should be deeply involved in efforts to engage employees in the change process through a variety of activities, which may vary from project to project and from organisation to organisation. The following is a collection of common activities that change champions may help facilitate:

Pre-strategy

- Vision workshops
- Co-creation workshops
- Lessons-learnt workshops
- Establishing a change roadmap

Post-strategy

- Introduction workshops
- Training planning processes
- Key issues workshops
- All-hands meetings

There are other means to communicate with employees that change champions may not be involved with. Some of these include:

- Bulletins/emails
- Graphics and messages for use across micro-sites and construction sites
- Initiation visits during construction
- Upcoming change videos
- New ways of working playbook/digital info-pack

Driving Change through Leadership and a Toolkit

While change champions play a crucial role in disseminating and socialising change within their teams, it is pertinent to note that a significant portion of the process must be driven from the top. A designated figurehead like a CEO can act as a driving force behind the transformation. The figurehead's role extends beyond mere advocacy, encompassing active involvement in decision-making, communication and fostering a culture conducive to change acceptance. Leaders not only symbolise the organisational commitment to change but also act as a guiding force, ensuring coherence and alignment throughout the transformative journey. The figurehead's influence goes beyond individual teams, resonating across the entire organisation, reinforcing the importance and inevitability of the impending change.

Often a figurehead, surrounded by supportive change champions, is not enough. Time and time again, we have found that transformational change can only work if mid-managers are fully onboard and leading, standing side by side with the figurehead. This is because middle managers may feel that they have the most to lose through transformational change and might unintentionally undermine it. They may resist the change due to concerns about job security, alterations to established power dynamics or disruptions to familiar routines. To address this, it is imperative to engage middle managers proactively and address their concerns, ensuring they become advocates rather than potential saboteurs of the transformative process. Participative management means not just involving the grassroots employees. It can be just as important, if not more, to involve mid-level managers in all levels of transformational change.

What naturally follows is the process of choosing the right people from the middle-manager pool to be involved with workplace transformation. In some cases, it is best for top managers to simply make the choice about participants. In other cases, it may pay dividends for a group of middle managers to nominate someone experienced, preferably from the HR or FM departments, to drive the task force that will actually implement a plan.

What helps, no matter who is leading, is for all organisations to develop a change toolkit, a document that:

- Lists all possible activities
- Explains how each activity needs to be run, with details of ownership, frequency and preparation required
- Defines levels of intensity of change, mapping which activities need to be linked with each level of intensity

External help from change management consultants is recommended if an organisation is undergoing a major workplace transformation. Consultants can help with drafting a change toolkit, drawing up a change communication plan and facilitating the activities listed therein.

The world of work has undergone sea changes, especially during the COVID era. It was not easy for many employees to begin working from home. It has been even more difficult for them to return to work in offices. Such changes need to be managed. People only adapt well to change when they feel a strong sense of belonging to something that they co-created, especially when it is a difficult-to-complete transformation plan. However, it is essential to acknowledge that certain transformation programmes may be so impactful and far-reaching that centralised control from the upper echelons of the organisation becomes imperative. Striking a balance between fostering a collaborative, co-creative environment and exercising top-down leadership is crucial in orchestrating successful and sustainable transformations.

Integrate and Automate Building Services

Sensors and software too need to be piloted before a full roll-out. Integrating building services with sensors that pick up data about occupancy within the office and then automating the analysis of this data is gaining in popularity because of the variety of benefits it offers. Two benefits stand out:

Optimising energy use and reducing the carbon footprint: It makes complete sense, for example, to heat a room when someone is using it. Services like air conditioning and lighting can turn on only when the sensors know a room is occupied. Sensors that pick up real-time occupancy data across various spaces within an office or complex, in conjunction with software, help reduce energy bills by making sure the facilities are shut off or dialled down when they are not being used. So the lights or air conditioning of a room will only turn on when the sensors detect an occupant in the room.

Curating personalised experiences for employees through software: When sensors and employee apps are used to collect non-private data about the personal choices of employees, groups like the HR department can begin the process of analysing the data and personalising workplace experiences.

Imagine a day in the office for Mary, where ample natural light ensures she can work at her chosen desk without any artificial lighting. The blinds on the wide windows move based on the time of day, following the sun's movement across the sky as well as the weather. The blinds are run on automated motors operated from the cloud, based on ambient sunlight data picked up by sensors and weather information gathered from the internet. When it is almost time for her scheduled meeting with Ajay and Amy, she gets an alert on her phone app, reminding her fifteen minutes in advance about the location of the meeting room along with its description and ways to get to it. She is also informed that Ajay is unable to attend the meeting and is prompted to choose a smaller meeting room that is appropriate for a two-person meeting. The agenda of the meeting is also included in the brief in the app. As she walks towards the meeting room, she even gets an alert saying, 'Hey Mary, would you like to pick up some orange juice from the refreshment station located towards the right of the chosen meeting room?' She gets this, as the algorithm knows that Mary likes orange juice and that she usually gets something to drink before her meetings.

The degree of such automation and personalisation is limitless and is something that has to be a part of emerging workplace designs.

At times, a transformation initiative may involve only the integration and automation of existing building services with no other changes. Such integration doesn't always need to be done when a new office is being built. Transformation can be conducted independently in brownfield projects as well.

The image on the following page shows a simple workflow for pulling off such an integration in both brownfield and greenfield situations. The possibilities of customisation within each step are numerous. And yet, there are reasons for concern when certain brownfield projects lack interoperability or when a project faces disallowance of one system talking to another. When systems lack compatibility or face restrictions on communication, potential issues could include data silos, inefficiencies or disruptions in the seamless functioning of integrated technologies. Addressing these concerns becomes crucial to ensuring the success of transformative workplace solutions in diverse project scenarios.

Setting the issue of interoperability aside, let us look briefly at the possibilities with reference to the image on the next page.

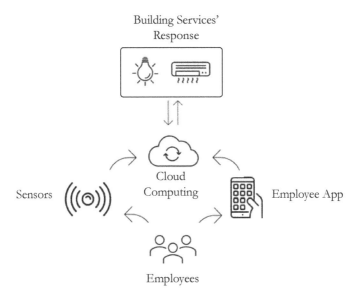

Integrating with Employee Apps

Along with providing various services for the physical office, such as the ability to book different workspaces, employee apps also create a wealth of data that can be used to curate personalised experiences. For example, let us say that Jack has booked a meeting room for an hour. Ten minutes before the meeting, Jack receives a message on his app asking, 'Would you like the room temperature for your next meeting at the Xanadu Room to be set at 72 degrees?' When he selects 'yes', he is presented with other options. The information about his preferences will be sent to the cloud for processing and storage. The processed data is used to send a request to the air conditioner in the Xanadu Room to be turned on three minutes before the meeting is scheduled to start.

So, what happens if Jack or other participants do not turn up for the meeting on time? Occupancy sensors in the room can be programmed to wait up to five minutes for the room to be occupied. If no one comes in, data from the sensor will be processed in the cloud, this time sending a message for the air conditioner to be switched off. This is where the cloud can integrate sensor data with employee data. This is a tricky area as employees may not want their every movement to be tracked. Hence only such data that is not considered private ought to be used.

Automation like this should be handled with care and ought to be driven with a motive to achieve transformation goals, instead of making employees seem lazy for not remembering to turn off lights when they leave a meeting room. A compelling change communication drive can be effective in encouraging employees to manually switch off lights and air conditioners when not required rather than investing in such automation. What is pertinent is that the automation possibilities are limitless today, especially when AI is added to the mix. Automation needs to be considered as a part of a holistic approach to adopting new ways of working and not as a standalone activity. It is only then that such automation will contribute meaningfully towards supporting an organisational workplace transformation.

Integrate Productivity and Collaboration Tools

The road to a future in which employees will spend time in metaverses will see a lot of stops and starts involving technology integration. The first step is integration between current digital workplace tools. The next step will be integration between the world of digital workplace tools and the physical world.

When employees were onboarded onto digital workplace platforms en masse, these included mainly productivity and collaboration tools to begin with. Add to that another layer of employee platforms that involved apps for booking work desks, finding parking, etc., and you have the average employee switching between applications and devices throughout a workday, highlighting the pressing necessity for a unified sign-in experience.

In addition to the challenges posed by multiple sign-ins and sign-outs across various applications and devices in a hybrid work setting, another issue prompting the need for a seamless single sign-in experience is the security and management of user credentials. With the proliferation of digital platforms, employees often resort to using multiple passwords or credentials across different applications, leading to security vulnerabilities and increased administrative overhead in managing access credentials. A move towards a unified sign-in not only streamlines the user experience but also enhances cybersecurity measures by centralising access control and authentication processes.

The conventional understanding of productivity tools is this— they should offer calendars, email, task management, time tracking, document management and other features that help employees efficiently manage their work on a day-to-day basis. On the other hand, collaboration tools empower employees to work together on projects from anywhere in the world. The COVID pandemic saw the coming together of productivity tools and collaboration tools, leading to platforms promising to cover both aspects.

The shift is towards cloud-based apps that streamline multiple accounts, apps and workflows. Integration of Microsoft Teams into the Office 365 platform is an example of an early attempt at integrating productivity tools and collaboration tools.

Integrate with the Physical Office

Of particular interest for workplace management stakeholders is the merging of physical spaces with digital spaces and the growing number of possibilities in this area. A solution like Zoom Rooms, from collaboration platform Zoom, enables in-person and remote participants to interact in real time. The physical Zoom Room in the office can be booked remotely. And from it, almost anything can be shared from the physical to the digital domain easily. Telepresence from Cisco, as previously discussed, has similarities and has been around for many years.

A tool like Microsoft Places, and its likely integration with the Office 365 platform, is heralding the coming together of the physical and the digital worlds. Such platforms will undergo rapid advancements in the months to come. It will not be much longer before our digital selves will be projected as holographic images in meeting rooms in the office. This will be one of the places where the metaverse will meet the physical world.

Working Together

One can also see, through the examples given, how HR is brought into the fray as well when imagining the integration of IT and FM. The potential is boundless when envisioning the development of a hybrid workplace that seamlessly combines both physical and digital elements.

The technological integration field calls for creativity to be developed from within an organisation. If one depends on suppliers, the costs can be incredibly high. Alternatively, if an organisation develops integration plans by developing its own talent using some consultants and investing in some technology, it is possible to move forward without exorbitant expenses.

Different tech suppliers have their own vision of how the future will play out. These visions may not always be in sync with an organisation's needs. Workplace management stakeholders should be clear about their transformation goals and explore the possibilities before zeroing in on exactly what technology to buy.

Ideation sessions with participation from top management, IT, FM and HR teams are helpful when it comes to aligning project goals. These meetings should definitely be held, it probably goes without saying, before commitments to certain types of technology are made. Once an organisation is aligned and its goals are clear, discussions can be had with worktech solution providers.

Integrate Food and Transportation Tools

Organisations that enable a higher degree of personalisation in the workplace through technology will have large competitive advantages in the future, especially as metaverses come to the workplace. Two features in employee apps warrant special mention. These, alternatively, grant the ability to manage one's meal choices when an employee is at work and give the opportunity to manage one's commute to and from work with ease. This is important because, as hybrid work becomes mainstream, the choice and availability of food and transport when employees do not follow the same work patterns daily becomes critical.

The fusion of workplace personalisation and technological advancements not only fortifies an organisation's competitive edge but also positions it as a vanguard in promoting sustainable practices amid evolving work landscapes.

Food

Everyone accepts that mobile devices have disrupted the way that we order and consume food. The growth of delivery players across the globe has brought greater choice and ease. The tech-savvy knowledge worker is often time-starved and expects the same efficiency of common food apps while in the office. An inspiring café in the office offering a wide choice may not be enough for an organisation to keep its employees happy about food. Employees want a 360-degree food experience, supported by the best of app-based tools. As organisations go down the path of curating experiences at the workplace, employees will begin to expect the ability to customise their food choices too. Progressive organisations will view the offering of more food choices through employee apps as a key differentiator when it comes to attracting and keeping talent.

While working with an employee app developer, it is recommended that food management be considered as a possible integration with the mother app. Such integration can bring the following advantages:

- Food options from the in-house cafeteria and outside restaurants
- Service at various times of the day. This will be particularly important as more employees exercise flexibility around the hours of the day they spend at the office
- Nutritional and health information that is shared electronically with employees
- Carbon footprint data about different food options, based on geo-location technology

These advantages primarily emphasise the positive impact on employees. However, the progressive integration of these benefits is extending to the employer side as well. The backend dashboard of such app offers valuable insights into the popularity of specific foods, enabling a strategic optimisation of culinary choices. This optimisation not only enhances the overall dining experience for employees but also addresses concerns related to the preparation of unpopular dishes that might lead to wastage.

Furthermore, the introduction of AI-powered waste bins in recent times have proven instrumental in curbing food waste within organisations. The interactive nature of these bins, which display the precise amount of food wasted when employees dispose of their leftovers, makes individuals more conscious of their actions. This heightened awareness prompts employees to be more discerning during meal selections, avoiding excess portions or items they don't enjoy. Simultaneously, the integration of AI cameras above the bins captures images each time a plate is emptied, generating a comprehensive data set over days and weeks. Leveraging this data, the AI system can identify popular and less favoured dishes, empowering kitchen management to refine menus and eliminate items prone to higher wastage.

These measures, which do not cost a fortune to implement, foster a more sustainable and efficient approach within organisational settings. The seamless integration of technology, such as AI-powered waste bins and analytics, showcases the potential for creating environmentally conscious workplaces that simultaneously enhance employee experiences. As organisations embrace these innovations, they pave the way for a future where both individual satisfaction and broader sustainability goals harmoniously coexist.

Transport

In the contemporary landscape, sustainability considerations within organisations encompass the environmental impact of transportation, a facet gaining prominence, particularly with the advent of hybrid work disrupting conventional routines. The ensuing irregularity poses challenges to the established norms of commuting, necessitating a nuanced approach to transportation sustainability.

Crucially, the optimisation of transportation options becomes imperative to mitigate the organisation's carbon footprint. This objective is attainable through a multifaceted approach that encompasses strategic planning and the integration of AI-based technology. By leveraging advanced technology, organisations can streamline transport options, enhancing operational efficiency and simultaneously contributing to environmental conservation. The implementation of these measures not only brings about much-needed sustainability but also instils a culture of responsibility and adaptability within the organisational framework.

The implications, however, extend beyond environmental impact. The optimisation of transportation aligns with a broader commitment to employee welfare. As hybrid work introduces unconventional schedules and workdays, efficient commuting solutions become paramount. The integration of AI-based technology facilitates seamless travel experiences for employees, even during odd hours and non-traditional workdays.

With hybrid work, employees, more than ever before, need to have the full breadth of commuting options available to them on their smartphones, since earlier commute patterns will no longer hold. Expectations around this are growing because when one is working remotely, going to work is very easy; you need to walk from your bedroom to the study and log in. As a result, organisations will need to make it as easy as possible for employees to get to the office in a time- and cost-effective manner. While customising employee apps, it is advisable that transport options are covered.

A well-designed transport feature built into the employee app will be able to list, during any time of the day, a recommended means of transport from point A to point B. This list will include a variety of transport options like rented bikes, trains, buses or cabs. If public transport is the employee's preferred means of transport, those options will appear first. If they want to control their means of transportation and own the whole process, the app will prioritise taking the car, walking to work or using the scooter. Each of these options can also be listed according to the day's weather.

If an employee opts to drive to the office, they will be guided along the way. When nearing the office, the app will show the closest available parking slot near the employee's desk for the day.

Alternatively, if an organisation has a shuttle service or an outsourced fleet of transport options dedicated to its employees, they can find the best option from within the app to access these too.

There are multiple advantages for employees in incorporating a transport feature into employee apps:

- This approach optimises cost savings
- It saves time by eliminating or reducing waits. The app can prioritise up-to-the-minute wait times for each form of transportation
- Since employee safety is a key concern, the app may even select options where female employees, for example, get assigned cabs driven by women

The stress of commuting, especially when it comes to hybrid work, is accentuated by irregular working days. Hours lost because of inefficient transport options can be very frustrating. When added up, bad commutes can translate to the equivalent of many missed workdays. Similarly, bad and irregular commutes can lead to employees being late for meetings and even put people in a bad mood and lower their productivity. We all know of someone who took up a job because of a good commute or left a job because of a bad one. Including a transport feature in employee apps can offer a strategic advantage to organisations in hiring and retaining talent.

Designing a Workplace Has a Whole New Meaning

Designing the workplace has a whole new meaning today. It is about designing the physical and digital environment for work; it is about designing the very way work needs to be conducted; it is about designing the day-to-day experience for employees. The field of designing digital environments is making good progress and is headed in the direction of ensuring highly curated experiences for employees. Because such curation is relatively easy in the digital world and as employees become more and more used to technology, they now increasingly expect easy ways to get things done. These expectations extend to transport, food and meetings. The experiences employees have need to be curated in ways in which the employee journey is frictionless, like a flawless user interface in a good mobile app.

Embracing a holistic approach to designing the workplace, encompassing both physical and digital realms, not only enhances the day-to-day experiences of employees but also holds the potential to significantly bolster an organisation's sustainability initiatives. This emphasis on digital efficiency inherently aligns with sustainability goals by optimising resource utilisation and reducing unnecessary waste. Consequently, the fusion of user-friendly digital environments with sustainable practices becomes a cornerstone of an organisational culture committed to creating an eco-conscious and supportive workplace.

Complete Pulse Studies and Course Corrections

A data-driven, pilot-oriented, prototyped approach to workplace transformation initiatives promises solutions that are most likely to work well for the users. This type of approach involves being human-centric, capturing user aspirations and aligning those with the leadership's vision. But how do we know if the solution that is piloted is successful or not?

Criteria for Success and Pulse Studies

While gathering data about the leadership's vision and user aspirations, it is critical to establish the success criteria of the initiative. Success could mean energy savings, an increase in productivity, improved health, better talent retention or a combination of some of these and others. Criteria for success will differ based on the needs of leaders and employees.

A good initiative involves taking advantage of employee surveys and leadership interviews and conducting pulse studies three to six months after deploying a pilot. Pulse studies help determine:

- What worked and what did not
- Whether the pilot was considered a success by employees
- Areas for improvement
- Readiness for full deployment
- Whether one more pilot needs to be done before full deployment.

Pulse studies, as the name suggests, measure on-the-ground feelings about changes being rolled out through the pilot(s). If something in the pilot is not working, the pulse study will help an organisation determine a course correction that is likely to work. A quick pulse study may be enough in some instances, but that may not be enough when it comes to the sustained impact and long-term viability of the initiative beyond immediate feedback. Sometimes an in-depth analysis of how the initiative aligns with the leadership's vision and addresses both leaders' and employees' evolving needs may need to be conducted.

Within three to six months of the pilot roll-out, a mix of activities needs to be considered to follow up on a major initiative. Some of them are:

Employee surveys to gather feedback: The questionnaire needs to be designed in a way that it links back to identified criteria for success.

Focus groups: These need to cover the change champions because they are expected to be the eyes and ears on the ground and understand the pulse well. Such focus groups often uncover what employees really feel.

Observation studies: Observation studies help gauge employee behaviours, workstyles and how the infrastructure is working out.

Leadership interviews: Interviews with senior leadership help determine levels of success from a different perspective.

Functional reviews: Functional reviews uncover how key functions like HR, IT and FM are working in the new environment.

Pulse studies are a concise type of research. Knowledge is drawn from the data collated. Conclusions are reached. If further course corrections are required, they are made. And if necessary, pulse studies are repeated after a quarter. An example of how pulse studies are used was seen during the COVID pandemic, when many organisations repeated employee surveys to track various aspects of their physical and psychological health.

Valuable Feedback

In our work with clients, employees have expressed feeling valued and heard when they get the opportunity to provide feedback through pulse surveys. Participation in surveys and focus groups is high and effective if employees are engaged in the co-creation of the piloted solutions. The feedback coming out of the studies is very helpful because it:

- Acts as an early warning system if success metrics are not being met
- Helps measure the effectiveness of what pilots set out to achieve
- Assists in the process of discovering gaps (if any)

When these studies are done regularly, they end up becoming valuable tools. They are a means of bringing the voice of employees into the decision-making process. This is good for employees' sense of ownership and is good for an organisation.

Accumulate User Data to Help Personalise Experiences

The new ways of working being piloted may include an updated employee app and/or sensors capturing data. The data flowing out of these are very valuable and need to be analysed as part of pulse studies along with other data being generated. There are two aspects that need to be checked at the pulse-study stage:

1. How well are the sensors and/or the apps performing?
2. What are the occupancy and employee behavioural and workstyle trends emerging out of transformation process?

Performance

Suppliers of worktech solutions commit to certain performance standards. At the tail end of pilots, it is important to reflect on the actual performance of the solutions vs what was promised. We have talked about gaps already, especially regarding what internal teams can do. But it is also important to identify gaps, if any, in the work done by contractors. It is far better to do this analysis in the pilot stage rather than waiting until a roll-out is complete.

For purely IT-related performance, of course, it is the IT team that needs to do this audit. If any component includes amalgamation with the fit-out or with the building services, the FM team needs to be involved. Similarly, any external help received from MEP consultants needs to be judged by this same team.

Trends

Sensors and apps generate a wide range of data sets. Looking at trends in the variables within the data after six months of deployment is useful. Analysing any data produced should provide a clear picture of what is working well and what is not. However, one must not view such data in isolation, as it tells only half the story. Insights need to be viewed in combination with people data emerging out of other activities like pulse surveys and focus groups to get the real picture.

Fine-tune User Experiences

Throughout the previous chapters, we have been writing about making work easier. We have stressed that it is important to collect data about the behaviours and preferences of workers. That is because the average worker spends more and more time online. And it is there where experiences can be best tailored to suit the needs of the employees. As employees get used to such curation and move towards working in the metaverse, the need to curate experiences will only increase. Such experiences that can be done only if management has access to real-time and historical data about employees' choices.

The deployment of a pilot, as outlined in the preceding chapters, underscores the significance of user experiences, utilising data harvested during the initial phases. These early datasets provide insights into the thoughts and expectations of individuals before the full implementation of the resultant solution.

Examining the data sets one to six months post-pilot deployment becomes an invaluable lens through which to observe and understand the work dynamics and behavioural patterns of employees within the context of the new workplace and evolving methodologies. This perspective over time provides a thorough comprehension of how the workforce engages with the altered environment and adjusts to innovative work methodologies. It enables management to stay attuned to the pulse of employees, fostering a work environment that is not just adaptive but anticipatory of the workforce's evolving needs and preferences.

IMPLEMENT

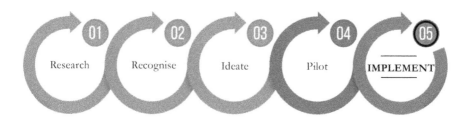

01 Research | 02 Recognise | 03 Ideate | 04 Pilot | 05 IMPLEMENT

Roll Out

A pilot provides valuable information. Based on the learnings from pulse studies, the workplace management team may decide to go back to the drawing board to fine-tune things. Once ready, transformation solutions are rolled out across multiple locations or the entire workplace.

Real-time data from employee apps and sensors can be used to effect real-time action, thereby curating rich user experiences. In an earlier chapter, we narrated a futuristic story about Mike and his workplace journey when his organisation moved to the metaverse. Although we are a few years away from that world, most of the technology required for that journey is already here. Over the next few years, most of it is expected to integrate. So organisations will benefit much from a prototyping-piloting-full roll-out approach as the metaverse arrives in workplaces.

Regional Variations

While pilots help weed out problems common before a full roll-out, standardised roll-outs driven from headquarters, even after prototypes and pilots, at times face regional challenges. For organisations that have a presence in multiple locations with very different cultures, it is critical that the roll-out strategy has built-in flexibility to allow regional variations. For example, we have witnessed that the effectiveness of standardised hybrid work policies has wildly different outcomes, especially when companies have offices in multiple countries. These different outcomes can be caused by variables as simple as the availability or unavailability of a good public transportation system or diversity in cultural preferences around privacy. Smart workplace management leaders leave space for regional flexibility around roll-outs.

Managing User Proficiency in Transformations

As organisations progress beyond the initial pilot stage and commence the operationalisation of transformative elements, such as automated building services and employee apps, it becomes imperative to fortify these advancements with a robust change management initiative. Despite substantial financial investments in cutting-edge technology, there exists a common oversight—a failure to adequately familiarise users with the new technology, spaces and operational paradigms. The discrepancy between implementation and user assimilation can impede the seamless adoption of these innovations. This is where a comprehensive change management strategy steps in, acting as a guiding force to bridge the gap between technological evolution and user proficiency.

The complexity lies not only in the integration of novel

technologies but also in cultivating an environment where employees feel adept and at ease within the transformed workspace. Frequently, organisations allocate significant budgets to acquire state-of-the-art solutions, yet the oversight of user orientation persists. The value of a well-informed and comfortable workforce cannot be overstated in the success of these technological endeavours. Hence, a multifaceted approach to change management becomes paramount, comprising various initiatives such as townhall sessions, informative bulletins, user playbooks and targeted training sessions.

Townhall sessions serve as platforms for transparent communication, deciphering the rationale behind the technological shifts and addressing any concerns or queries. Informative bulletins disseminate crucial information, updates and procedural guidelines, ensuring a continuous flow of knowledge. User playbooks act as comprehensive guides, explaining the functionalities and intricacies of the new technologies, thereby empowering employees to navigate the transformed landscape with confidence. Simultaneously, training sessions, tailored to the specific needs of the workforce, provide hands-on experience and practical insights, fostering a culture of continuous learning.

In essence, the journey from technological implementation to user proficiency necessitates more than just the introduction of cutting-edge tools; it demands a concerted effort to nurture a workplace culture in which adaptation and proficiency fuse seamlessly. The integration of technology should not be an isolated endeavour but a holistic transformation that aligns the workforce with the evolving dynamics of the modern workplace.

Revitalise

Organisations saw the learnings from the pandemic as a huge opportunity to bring about course corrections in the way they function. Given the almost universal acceptance that remote work is going to be an integral part of future operations, many organisations used the pandemic to rejig their workplace practices and designs. This allowed the physical office to undergo changes mid-way through lease contract periods. Although the COVID years were different in every other way, making changes in how people work mid-way though short lease periods was also unique. As changes are expensive, organisations traditionally wait about three years or so after a new workplace is established before embarking on changes. However, given the volatile times we live in nowadays, organisations often eliminate the need to wait for the lease period to expire or for something catastrophic to happen to make changes.

The trendy managerial acronym VUCA, short for volatility, uncertainty, complexity and ambiguity, summarises the current world. Business requirements change and the office may need to expand or contract suddenly. When such situations arise, it is a good opportunity to go back to the drawing board and analyse learnings. By following the steps explained in the previous chapters, it is likely to be easier to make changes on the fly because, first, you will be familiar with the process and, second, you will have access to the roadmap we provided to help you use big data from employee apps, sensors and dashboards. This data will provide the evidence needed to take quick informed decisions.

Evaluation

The journey does not culminate with the initial transformation. The crucial phase of evaluation looms large as organisations transition into the roll-out phase and beyond. Revisiting the meticulous steps outlined in the pilot sections becomes imperative, serving as the foundation for successful roll-outs and sustained improvements. The cyclical nature of organisational growth demands complete reviews of major initiatives to track performance, extract learnings and refine processes. Continuous learning and adaptation emerge as the cornerstones of a resilient and agile future.

As organisations navigate the complexities of multiple workplace transformations throughout their lifetimes, the importance of holistic evaluations cannot be overstated. The wisdom derived from scrutinising each phase, from initiation to pilot to roll-out, positions organisations not merely as survivors but as architects of their destiny. The journey outlined in these pages serves as a testament to the capacity for organisations to evolve, innovate and thrive in the face of uncertainty. By embracing change as a constant and leveraging the insights gleaned from each transformation, organisations are empowered to forge ahead into an era where agility and adaptability define success.

Conclusion

While completing the research that informed this book, we came across science and evidence to support many of the points we have made. But there is no paper, book or university course that focuses on the relationships between each of the topics. There are great resources out there that touch on individual parts of what we have written about, but nothing connects all the dots. This is because the need to connect the dots has emerged only in recent years. The process began during the worst of the COVID pandemic. Slowly, this book took shape as we saw distinct links between the parts. The final version leverages tested methodologies and explains, through easy-to-understand steps, how to pull it all together.

The years encompassing and following the COVID pandemic have underscored the heightened significance that organisations attribute to two pivotal realms: the well-being of their employees, viewed from the employer's perspective, and the sustainability of the environment, scrutinised from the organisational standpoint. Within the pages of our book, we contend that the forthcoming adoption of worktech solutions and various technological advancements within organisations is inevitable due to impending tectonic shifts, ultimately leading to a scenario where employees find themselves working in the metaverse.

In the sweeping wave of technology integration, our emphasis lies in the assertion that technological solutions should not be mere off-the-shelf acquisitions; instead, they demand a nuanced approach involving customisation. This customisation is twofold—it caters to the overarching needs of the organisation while also possessing the adaptability to customise solutions for individual users. The core outcome of this tailored approach is profound: technology becomes a tool for optimising not only employee happiness and well-being but also concurrently streamlining and enhancing the utilisation of organisational resources and assets.

This strategic approach yields a dual benefit, acting as a catalyst for the genuine fulfilment of both employee well-being and organisational sustainability goals. Unlike superficial greenwashing and sloganeering efforts, this approach brings about tangible progress. When successfully implemented, it transforms the brand image of an organisation, rendering it more attractive and competitive. Consequently, organisations become adept at not only attracting but also retaining top talent, as the comprehensive care for the well-being of employees and the earnest pursuit of sustainability goals resonate deeply with individuals seeking purpose and commitment in their professional engagements.

However, every organisation is different. Not only are organisational goals different but the aspirations of employees are also unique. The steps described here should not be considered as magic bullets that will work for all organisations. Our book is written in such a way that you can pick up elements that are suitable for you and then create a formula that will fulfil your organisation's goals.

We wrote this book keeping in mind all stakeholders involved in workplace transformation initiatives. We thought it important that the book be accessible to consultants, designers, tech suppliers and service providers, among others. Most importantly, we want the book to be used by organisational leaders. We want to help people better understand the interconnectedness between issues and disciplines we discuss. Easy Work is work in progress and is theoretically limitless.

We encourage you to share your thoughts, ideas and relevant examples with us. Through this process, we will be able to keep growing and developing ideas and solutions to problems that you may consider to be more pressing for your organisations.

—Parthajeet, John and Raj

✉   connect@easywork.space
💻   www.EasyWork.space

References

1. Devon Delfino, 'How Musicians Really Make Their Money—and It Has Nothing to Do with How Many Times People Listen to Their Songs', *Business Insider*, 20 November 2018, https://www. businessinsider.in/tech/how-musicians-really-make-their-money-and-it-has-nothing-to-do-with-how-many-times-people-listen-to-their-songs/articleshow/66288613.cms. Accessed on 20 December 2023.
2. Cell Press, 'Pure Novelty Spurs the Brain', *Science Daily*, 27 August 2006, http://www.sciencedaily.com/releases/2006/08/060826180547. htm. Accessed on 20 December 2023.
3. Thierry Steimer, 'The Biology of Fear and Anxiety-Related Behaviors', *Dialogues in Clinical Neuroscience*, September 2002, 4(3): 231–49, doi: 10.31887/DCNS.2002.4.3/tsteimer. PMC Pub Med Central, https://www.ncbi.nlm.nih.gov/pmc/articles/PMC3181681/. Accessed on 20 December 2023.
4. Belle Beth Cooper, 'Novelty and the Brain: Why New Things Make Us Feel So Good', *Life Hacker*, 21 May 2013, https:// lifehacker.com/novelty-and-the-brain-why-new-things-make-us-feel-so-g-508983802. Accessed on 20 December 2023.
5. Allie Caren, 'Why We Remember the Bad Better Than the Good', *The Washington Post*, 1 November 2018, https://www.washingtonpost. com/science/2018/11/01/why-we-often-remember-bad-better-than-good/. Accessed on 21 December 2023.

6. Tim Burton (Director), *Charlie and the Chocolate Factory* (Film), Warner Bros, 2005.

7. Rudiger Ahrend et al., 'Changes in the Geography Housing Demand After the Onset of COVID-19: First Results from Large Metropolitan Areas in 13 OECD Countries', *OECD Economics Department Working Papers, No. 1713.* OECD Publishing, Paris. https://doi.org/10.1787/9a99131f-en, https://www.oecd.org/publications/changes-in-the-geography-housing-demand-after-the-onset-of-covid-19-first-results-from-large-metropolitan-areas-in-13-oecd-9a99131f-en.htm. Accessed on 21 December 2023.

8. B. Joseph Pine II and James H. Gilmore, 'Welcome to the Experience Economy', *Harvard Business Review*, July–August 1998, https://hbr.org/1998/07/welcome-to-the-experience-economy. Accessed on 21 December 2023.

9. Steven Miles, *The Experience Society: Consumer Capitalism Rebooted*, Pluto Press, 2021.

10. Gerhard Schulze, *The Experience Society*, SAGE Publications, 2008.

11. Harris Poll, *Millennials: Fueling the Experience Economy*, Eventbrite, July 2014, https://eventbrite-s3.s3.amazonaws.com/. Accessed on 21 December 2023. Marketing/Millennials_Research/Gen_PR_Final.pdf

12. 'The Deloitte Millennial Survey', *Deloitte*, January 2014, https://www2.deloitte.com/content/dam/Deloitte/global/Documents/About-Deloitte/gx-dttl-2014-millennial-survey-report.pdf Accessed on 28 December 2023.

13. Paris Stevens, 'The 2021 Workplace Friendship & Happiness Survey', *Wildgoose*, 19 July 2021, https://wearewildgoose.com/usa/news/workplace-friendship-and-happiness-survey/. Accessed on 21 December 2023.

14. Valerie Bolden-Barret, 'Millennials Seek Meaning at Work-and Employers Can Help', *HR Dive*, 30 October 2019, https://www.hrdive.com/news/millennials-seek-meaning-at-work-and-employers-can-help/566118/. Accessed on 21 December 2023.

15. Roula Amire and Great Place to Work, 'The Best Workplaces for Millennials Offer Meaning and Purpose', *Fortune*, 18 July 2022, https://fortune.com/2022/07/18/best-workplaces-millennials-2022-purpose-meaning/. Accessed on 21 December 2023.

16. Mike Rendall et al., 'Millennials at Work: Reshaping the Workplace', November 2011, PWC. https://www.pwc.com/co/es/publicaciones/assets/millennials-at-work.pdf. Accessed on 21 December 2023.

17. '2021 Employee Experience Survey', *Willis Towers Watson*, 20 July 2021, https://www.wtwco.com/en-US/Insights/2021/07/2021-employee-experience-survey. Accessed on 21 December 2023.

18. Dominika Kowalska, 'Who Can You Trust at Work? [2022 Study]', *ResumeLab*, 27 April 2022, https://resumelab.com/career-advice/trust-at-work. Accessed on 21 December 2023.

19. Lydia Dishman, 'Why Employees Don't Trust Their Leadership', *Fast Company*, 6 April 2016, https://www.fastcompany.com/3058630/why-employees-dont-trust-their-leadership. Accessed on 21 December 2023.

20. Clayton M. Christensen, *The Innovator's Dilemma: When New Technologies Cause Great Firms to Fail*, Harvard Business School Press, 1997.

21. 'News Release, Bureau of Labor Statistics, USDL-22-1758', NBC News, 30 August 2022, https://www.bls.gov/news.release/pdf/jolts.pdf. Accessed on 21 December 2023.

22. Abhinav Chugh, 'What Is "The Great Resignation"? An Expert Explains', *World Economic Forum*, 29 November 2021, https://www.weforum.org/agenda/2021/11/what-is-the-great-resignation-and-what-can-we-learn-from-it/. Accessed on 21 December 2023.

23. Geoff Colvin, 'Goldman Sachs Is Ordering Employees Back to the Office 5 Days (or More) a Week', 11 March 2022, *Fortune*, https://fortune.com/2022/03/10/goldman-sachs-office-hybrid-remote-work-david-solomon/. Accessed on 21 December 2023.

24. Daniella Silva, 'Coronavirus Has Lifted the Work-from-Home Stigma. How Will That Shape the Future?', *NBC News*, 13 May

2020, https://www.nbcnews.com/news/us-news/coronavirus-has-lifted-work-home-stigma-how-will-shape-future-n1205376. Accessed on 21 December 2023.

25. Jane Haskell, 'Working Agreements', *The University of Maine*, https://www.uvm.edu/sites/default/files/working-agreements-defined.pdf. Accessed on 21 December 2023.

26. Rosabeth Moss Kanter, 'Ten Reasons People Resist Change', *Harvard Business Review*, 25 September 2012, https://hbr.org/2012/09/ten-reasons-people-resist-chang. Accessed on 21 December 2023.

27. Kelsey Miller, '5 Critical Steps in the Change Management Process', *Harvard Business School Online*, 19 March 2020, https://online.hbs.edu/blog/post/change-management-process. Accessed on 21 December 2023.

28. Jared Spataro, 'Introducing Microsoft Places: Turn Your Spaces into Places', *Microsoft 365 Blog*, 12 October 2022, https://www.microsoft.com/en-us/microsoft-365/blog/2022/10/12/introducing-microsoft-places-turn-your-spaces-into-places/. Accessed on 21 December 2023.

29. 'Metaverse Market Size, Share & COVID-19 Impact Analysis', *Fortune Business Insights*. https://www.fortunebusinessinsights.com/metaverse-market-106574. Accessed on 21 December 2023.

30. Bryan Robinson, 'Remote Work Is Here to Stay and Will Increase into 2023, Experts Say', *Forbes*, 1 February 2022, https://www.forbes.com/sites/bryanrobinson/2022/02/01/remote-work-is-here-to-stay-and-will-increase-into-2023-experts-say/?sh=14da53cc20a6. Accessed on 21 December 2023.

31. '25 Percent of All Professional Jobs in North America Will Be Remote by End of Next Year', *Ladders*, 7 December 2021, https://www.theladders.com/press/25-of-all-professional-jobs-in-north-america-will-be-remote-by-end-of-next-year. Accessed on 21 December 2023.

32. 'Roger Walcott Sperry', *Wikipedia*,https://en.wikipedia.org/wiki/Roger_Wolcott_Sperry. Accessed on 21 December 2023.

33. Eagle Gamma, 'Left Brain vs Right Brain', *Simply Psychology*,

18 May 2021, https://www.simplypsychology.org/left-brain-vs-right-brain.html. Accessed on 21 December 2023.

34. Ashu Goel, 'The Rise of the Right-Brained Organization', *Forbes*, 28 May 2022, https://www.forbes.com/sites/forbesbusiness developmentcouncil/2020/05/28/the-rise-of-the-right-brained-organization/?sh=537770fb7bba. Accessed on 21 December 2023.

35. John Spacey, '11 Examples of Ease of Use', *Simplicable*, 14 August 2017, https://simplicable.com/new/ease-of-use; Mareike Bönninger, 'How Will Changing Workplace Behaviors Define the Future of Work?', *EY*, 14 March 2022, https://www.ey.com/en_no/consulting/how-will-changing-workplace-behaviors-define-the-future-of-work. Accessed on 21 December 2023.

36. B.J. Fogg, 'A Behavior Model for Persuasive Design', Standford University, 2009 https://drive.google.com/file/d/19LYba4fuceGM 3KhqxTXByV4msmb33t1o/view. Accessed on 21 December 2023.

37. 'The Fogg Behavior Model: A Framework for Behavior Change', *Growth Engineering*, 9 March 2020, https://www.growthengineering. co.uk/bj-foggs-behavior-model/. Accessed on 21 December 2023.

38. 'The Fogg Behavior Change Model: A Simple Summary', *World of Work Project*, https://worldofwork.io/2019/04/the-fogg-behavior-model/. Accessed on 21 December 2023.

39. Janelle de Weerd, 'Master the Fogg Behavior Model for eCommerce Persuasive Design', *Crobox*, 29 November 2017, https://blog.crobox. com/article/fogg-behavior-model. Accessed on 21 December 2023.

40. 'Persuasive Technology', *Wikipedia*, https://en.wikipedia.org/wiki/ Persuasive_technology. Accessed on 21 December 2023.

41. Jeff Orlowski (Director), *The Social Dilemma* (Film), Exposure Labs, 2020.

42. Alex Hern, 'Netflix's Biggest Competitor? Sleep', *The Guardian*, 18 April 2017, https://www.theguardian.com/technology/2017/ apr/18/netflix-competitor-sleep-uber-facebook. Accessed on 21 December 2023.

43. Tristan Harris, Center for Humane Technology, https://www. tristanharris.com/. Accessed on 21 December 2023.

44. Wayne Parker, 'The Risks and Dangers of Snapchat for Teens', *VeryWell Family*, 3 June 2022, https://www.verywellfamily.com/what-is-snapchat-and-its-use-1270338. Accessed on 21 December 2023.

45. Tristan Harris, 'Our Brains Are No Match for Our Technology', 5 December 2019, *The New York Times*, https://www.nytimes.com/2019/12/05/opinion/digital-technology-brain.html. Accessed on 21 December 2023.

46. Jeff Horvath, 'Persuasive Design: It's Not Just About Selling Stuff', in Aaron Marcus, Elizabeth Rosenzweig, and Marcelo M. Soares (eds), *Design, User Experience, and Usability*, Springer, 2011.

47. Richard H. Thaler and Cass R. Sunstein, *Nudge: Improving Decisions About Health, Wealth, and Happiness*, Penguin Books, 2009.

48. Devangi Vivrekar, 'Persuasive Design Techniques in the Attention Economy: User Awareness, Theory, and Ethics', Stanford University, 6 June 2018, https://stacks.stanford.edu/file/druid:rq188wb9000/Masters_Thesis_Devangi_Vivrekar_2018.pdf. Accessed on 22 December 2023.

49. 'You're Not the Boss of Me! Why We Don't Like Being Told What to Do', *Cleveland Clinic*, 17 November 2020, https://health.clevelandclinic.org/why-we-dont-like-being-told-what-to-do/. Accessed on 22 December 2023.

50. 'What is Ease of Use', *IGI Gobal*. https://www.igi-global.com/dictionary/ease-of-use/8997. Accessed on 22 December 2023.

51. 'How to Design for Ease of Use', *Interaction Design Foundation*, https://www.interaction-design.org/literature/article/how-to-design-for-ease-of-use. Accessed on 22 December 2023.

52. Frank Spillers, 'How to Explain Ease of Use vs Context of Use to Your Boss', *Experience Dynamics*, 17 January 2020. https://www.experiencedynamics.com/blog/2020/01/how-explain-ease-use-vs-context-use-your-boss. Accessed on 22 December 2023.

53. Redaction Blog, 'Airbnb, Spearheading the Employee Experience', *Coorp Academy*, 2019, https://www.coorpacademy.com/en/

blog/learning-innovation-en/airbnb-spearheading-the-employee-experience/. Accessed on 22 December 2023.

54. Max Meyers, Hannah Roth, Eric Niu, David A. Dye, 'Employees As Customers. Reimagining the Employee Experience in Government', *Deloitte Insights*, 31 May 2016, https://www2.deloitte.com/us/en/insights/industry/public-sector/treating-employees-as-customers-in-government.html. Accessed on 22 December 2023.

55. Kate Morgan, 'What's the Purpose of the Office—and Do We Still Need It?', *BBC*, 22 July 2021, https://www.bbc.com/worklife/article/20210721-whats-the-purpose-of-the-office-and-do-we-still-need-it. Accessed on 22 December 2023.

56. Laura Wright, 'How to Make Your Accounting Data Actionable', *OnePoint*, https://onepointaccounting.com/make-accounting-data-actionable/. Accessed on 22 December 2023.

Index

A

Advanced Workplace Associates, 99

agile work policy, 193

agile work, 50, 201

Airbnb, x, 17, 128

algorithm, 6, 60, 68, 84, 86–88, 94, 96, 119,138, 160, 167, 190, 208

Amazon, x, xii, 57, 89, 97, 114, 117

American dream, 21

amygdala, 6, 50

artificial intelligence (AI), ix, 35, 60, 65, 67–69, 72, 83, 89, 103, 117, 118, 139, 168, 189, 190–193, 210, 215–217

attract and retain talent, 9, 46

augmented reality (AR), xiv, 83, 85–89, 94, 117

avatar, 78–81, 86, 89, 91

B

baby boomer, 21–22

Bellas, Zach, 4

big data, xiv, 35, 65, 66–67, 69, 72, 83, 97, 131, 138–140, 166, 167–173, 229

Bloom, Nicholas, 39

Bock, Laszlo, 129

bricks, bytes and behaviours, 107

Brooks, Garth, 5

building management system (BMS), 87, 191–192

burnout, 36, 45

Burton, Tim, 10

Bush, Michael C., 22

Business Insider, 4

C

Cadence Innova, 241

Camus, Albert, 9

Center for Humane Technology, 114, 118

change communication plan, 53, 202–203, 206

change management, xvi, 28, 49, 50–59, 103, 107, 145, 149, 193, 198, 200–201, 206, 227–228

Charlie and the Chocolate Factory, 10

ChatGPT, ix, 68, 89

Christensen, Clayton, 31

Cisco, 192–193, 212

consumption of experiences, 16
Cooper, Belle Beth, 6
COVID-19, ix, x, 13, 25, 31, 35,
	37, 51, 64, 74, 94, 128, 129,
	131, 174, 193, 206, 211, 221,
	229, 231

D
Deliveroo, x
Dell, 177–179
digital profile, xiv
Dixon, Mark, 135
Duzel, Dr Emrah, 6

E
ease of use, xiii, 56, 57, 60, 84, 90,
	92, 103, 104, 108, 110–111,
	113, 115–116, 127
Edelman, 27
Einstein, Albert, 180
employee app, xiv, 9, 26, 29, 45,
	58, 63, 64, 103, 120, 133,
	139, 146, 157, 165, 168,
	169–173, 175, 179, 181, 198,
	207, 209–210, 214–215, 217,
	223, 226, 227, 229
employee health & safety (EHS),
	162
employee survey, 33, 43, 157, 160,
	161, 176, 180, 197, 220, 221
Eras Tour, 4, 5
Eventbrite, 17
experience economy, 15, 16, 17,
	18
experience journey, xv, 8, 26, 28,
	29, 62, 72, 130, 133, 138,
	156, 171
experience society, 15–20, 31

F
Facebook, 73, 78, 114, 121
fear of missing out (FOMO), 18,
	109, 113
five human senses, 4
focus group, 28, 53, 131, 133, 137,
	147, 160, 163, 176, 179, 202,
	221, 222, 224
Fogg Behaviour Model, 107–113,
	114, 116
Fogg, B.J., 108
food choice, 45, 63, 87, 103, 139,
	214
Forrester, 174
Fortune, 22, 38, 79
Freespace, 77, 241

G
Gen Z, 14, 17, 18–19, 21, 60, 93
Goel, Ashu, 96
Goldman Sachs, 38
Google, 68, 76, 90, 117, 129
Great Place to Work, 22
Great Resignation, 35–36
green consultant, 189
Gucci, 90

H
Harris, Tristan, 114, 118, 119, 121
Harvard Business Review, 15, 50
Haskell, Jane, 47
Hastings, Reed, 116
hippocampus, 6
Horvath, Jeff, 122
HR manager, 36, 91, 102, 133,
	175, 203
hybrid work policy, 37, 46, 47,
	120, 181, 184, 193, 198, 227

hybrid work, xi, 31, 32–33, 38, 58, 61, 62, 75, 76, 80, 81–83, 91, 93, 121, 125, 133, 136, 154, 192, 196, 211, 214, 216, 217, 218

I

immersive virtual world, xiv
in-office working, xi
insights, 76, 97, 132, 137, 147, 148, 157, 161, 163, 166, 170, 173, 174–179, 191, 198, 215, 224, 228, 230
Instagram, 114
integrated building management system (IBMS), 191
interior designer, 88, 137, 186, 189, 193
International Workplace Group, 135
internet of things (IoT), 65, 69–71, 72, 139, 191
interoperability, 72–73, 76, 80, 208
interview, xv, 28, 131, 133, 137, 157–159, 160, 161–163, 165, 172, 177, 198, 220, 221

K

Kanter, Rosabeth Moss, 50
knowledge worker, ix, xi, xvii, 26, 31–32, 62, 73, 81, 84, 90, 91, 93, 94, 96, 99, 102, 125, 134, 214

L

Ladders, 81
layout, 158, 184, 186, 190, 195, 196, 198

leadership, 29, 34, 43–44, 65, 130, 132, 137, 143, 147, 160, 161–163, 179, 184, 199, 205–206, 220–221
Levy, Mark, 128
location choice, 44

M

machine learning, 65, 67–69, 191
Maine University, 47
Maslow, Abraham, 11
Matrix, The, 78
MEP (mechanical, engineering and plumbing), 189, 190, 193, 223
Meta, 89, 90, 116
Metallica, 5
metaverse, xiv, 26, 33, 77, 79–98, 99, 116–117, 121–122, 125, 192, 211–212, 214, 224, 226, 231
Microsoft 365, 75–76
Microsoft Places, 75–77, 117, 212
Microsoft Teams, 74, 212
Miles, Steven, 15
Miller, Kelsey, 52
moonlighting, 45

N

Netflix, 15, 17, 57, 97, 116, 117, 167–168
neuroscientist, 6, 95
new ways of working, 42, 49, 52, 55, 56, 107, 136, 156, 193, 198, 199, 201, 204, 210, 223
Nikeland, 79
Nobel Prize, 95
novelty, 5, 6–7, 9, 17, 35, 49, 54, 84, 101, 103, 114

O

one-click buy, xii
online collaboration, 57
online meeting, xi, 9, 177
Oxford University, 3

P

pandemic, ix, x, xi, 13, 15, 25, 27,
     28, 31, 32, 33, 35, 37, 38, 39,
     42, 51, 58, 62, 82, 94, 128, 131,
     174, 211, 221, 229, 231
PayPal, 73
people data, 97, 131, 133, 137,
     160, 202, 224
persuasive design, 114–126, 130,
     180
Persuasive Tech Lab, 119
physical infrastructure, 60–65, 72,
     78, 165
physical world, xiv, xv, 91–92,
     94–95, 97, 98, 117, 125, 211,
     212
Plum, Karen, 99–100
psychological, 4, 7, 11, 12, 15, 49,
     116, 119, 222
pulse studies, 220–223, 226
purpose, 19, 22–23, 29, 76, 94,
     101, 122, 135, 138, 139, 145,
     153, 189, 197, 232
PwC, 23

R

real estate efficiency, 32, 131
real estate portfolio, 132, 184, 186,
     188
reframe, 180–182
remote work, xi, 131, 136, 165,
     186, 229

remote worker, 75, 78, 83, 128
ResumeLab, 27
return to work, 51, 206
Roblox, 79

S

Schulze, Gerhard, 16
self-actualisation, 11, 13
sensor, xiv, 35, 70–71, 72, 86, 112,
     120, 131, 138, 160, 165, 168,
     169–170, 172–173, 175, 179,
     181, 191, 195, 207, 209, 223,
     226, 229
Simplicable, 104
small data, xv, 35, 97, 131,
     136–138, 160–166, 173
SMB Records, 5
Snapchat, 114, 118
Snow Crash, 78
Social Dilemma, The, 114
social media platform, xiii, 6, 16,
     79, 83, 114, 115, 118, 121
social media, xiii, 6, 18, 79, 114,
     116, 117, 121, 134, 138
socialisation, 138
Sperry, Roger Wolcott, 95
Stanford University, 8, 39, 108,
     119, 124
Stephenson, Neal, 78
substantia nigra, 6
survey, 27, 34–35, 39, 43, 53, 102,
     103, 120–121, 131, 133, 137,
     147, 166, 175, 181, 197
Swift, Taylor, 4, 5

T

Telepresence, 192, 212
Tesla, 73

three Bs, 107
TikTok, 114
toolkit, 205–206
touchpoint, xv, 8–9, 26, 29, 49,
    63, 73, 94, 95, 97, 102, 117,
    125, 127, 131, 133, 134, 136,
    156, 157
trend analysis, 64, 132, 140, 169,
    170, 173
trust, 9, 22, 27, 41, 116, 129, 154

U
U2, 5
Uberisation, 5
US Bureau of Labor Statistics,
    36
user experience, 59, 127, 158, 169,
    211, 224–225, 226

V
ventral segmental area, 6
virtual coffee, 28, 33, 74
virtual reality, xiv, 78
virtual working, xiv
Vivrekar, Devangi, 124
VUCA, 229

W
wellbeing, 27, 34, 40–41, 45, 65,
    146, 177, 178, 179, 231, 232
Wildgoose, 19
Willis Towers Watson, 27
Willy Wonka, 10
WinWire Technologies, 96
work from home, 13, 39, 44, 46,
    81, 82
work setting, 44, 50, 54, 81, 211
work timing, 44
work–life balance, 9, 23, 32, 36,
    40, 42, 146
Workplace Evolutionaries, 65, 147
workplace strategist, 137, 186, 189,
    193
workplace technology, 57
worktech, 57–59, 60–71, 78–92,
    93, 94, 125, 213, 223, 231

X
X (Twitter), 114

Z
Zoom, 28, 31, 62, 74, 193, 212
Zuckerberg, Mark, 89

About the Authors

Parthajeet Sarma

Mumbai-based Parthajeet is a Chevening scholar and a workplace experience designer, focused on developing workplace strategies for client organisations via data-driven approaches. He follows through by handholding organisations with change management initiatives. Since the nineties, Parthajeet has been immersed in the realm of workplace transformation. In 2003, he founded boutique consultancy iDream, which has evolved from a focus on workplace design to a comprehensive workplace experience design practice. Given the collaborative and evolving nature of the discipline of workplace transformation, Parthajeet often collaborates with global consulting and service partners on projects. A graduate of Sir JJ College of Architecture, Parthajeet went on to complete an MBA. After years of industry experience, he was selected by the British Government to do a leadership programme on science and innovation at the University of Oxford.

John Hoffmire

Oxford-based John is chairman of Cadence Innova, a change management consulting firm based in London. Before joining Saïd Business School at the University of Oxford and becoming the Director of the Center on Business and Poverty at the University of Wisconsin-Madison, John had a twenty-year career in equity investing, venture capital, consulting and investment banking. His work has had a particular focus on Employee Stock Ownership Plans. As founder and CEO of his own investment banking firm, he helped employees buy and manage approximately $2.2 billion worth of ESOPs. He sold his firm to American Capital, which then went public. John left American Capital as Senior Investment Officer when the company reached $1 billion in assets. After leaving American Capital, John was Vice President at Ampersand Ventures, formerly Paine Webber's private equity group. Earlier in his career, after he finished his PhD at Stanford University, he was a consultant at Bain & Company. John has written extensively about business and finance.

Raj Krishnamurthy

London-based Raj is the founder and CEO of Freespace, one of the fastest growing workplace technology solutions providers. Having earned an undergraduate degree from the Indian Institute of Technology, Bombay, and an MBA from Santa Clara University, Raj is experienced in delivering solutions for the workplace. He had previous roles as Innovations Director for a $1-billion sales facilities management company, and as General Manager of a $100-million sales global service organisation. He balances his passion for technology with creating value-based solutions that sustain for the long term. He is an expert in user-centric thinking solutions and systems.

Milton Keynes UK
Ingram Content Group UK Ltd.
UKHW020743140424
441032UK00012B/54/J

9 789360 453268